Successful Career Management

Strategies Beyond Technical Preparation

by
Robert Donald

Bloomington, IN Milton Keynes, UK

authorHOUSE

AuthorHouse™
1663 Liberty Drive, Suite 200
Bloomington, IN 47403
www.authorhouse.com
Phone: 1-800-839-8640

AuthorHouse™ UK Ltd.
500 Avebury Boulevard
Central Milton Keynes, MK9 2BE
www.authorhouse.co.uk
Phone: 08001974150

First published by AuthorHouse 5/6/2006

ISBN: 1-4259-0960-4 (sc)

Library of Congress Control Number: 2006900349

Printed in the United States of America
Bloomington, Indiana

This book is printed on acid-free paper.

Dedication

This book is dedicated to my parents, Earl and Carolyn Donald, for their unconditional love and support during my critically important developmental years. None of my career or personal achievements would have been possible without your guidance and daily positive examples. Thank you for stressing the importance of getting a good education, having a strong work ethic, being honest, respecting others, setting high goals and living a Christian life. I have more of an appreciation each day for the things you did and I pray that my life is a reflection of the many positive things you did continuously. My years of parent tapes are still functioning and I think about you daily.

Acknowledgements

I would like to acknowledge God for giving me the knowledge and initiative to complete this book. Without you, this would not have been possible. From day one, my intention was to provide insight to others in order to make their career endeavors more fruitful and I pray that I have accomplished that objective.

I would like to thank my wife, Elvah, for her patience and understanding while this effort was in the various stages of research and production. I am sure I was hard to live with during much of this time. In addition, your various business ventures over the years provided input that proved to be insightful, especially for areas associated with entrepreneurial endeavors.

Thank you, Mike Cooke for your inspirational and insightful input at various stages of the project. New thoughts emerged each time we talked and the ideas for career solutions kept coming. I would also like to thank Bert Elliott for his in-process input at various stages of the effort. Your input was valuable. The editorial and proof reading support received from Erika Anderson and Melwyn Turner respectively was just outstanding, and I thank you for your efforts.

I conducted surveys from professionals in various areas in order to get the value of diverse perspectives. The wisdom provided by this group proved to be an outstanding source of information. A special thank you to the following individuals for their input: Mr. Tom Adams, Mr. Robert Aston, Mrs. Phyllis Aston, Mr. Mike Cooke, Ms. Alison Brown, Mr. Michael Busser, Mrs. Elvah Donald, Ms. Mikki Donald, Mr. Martin Duncan, Mr. Bert Elliott, Dr. Robert Houston, Mr. Jerry Mills, Ms. Sherry Smith, Mr. Melwyn Turner, Dr. Rosalyn Vaughn, Mr. Dennis Vereb, Dr. Warren Wolf, Mr. Ned L. Womack. Also to all others who provided input but might have been inadvertently overlooked.

Table of Contents

Author's Note xi

Introduction xiii

Phase I: Career Selection and Decision Process 1
    Chapter One: Self-Assessment and Your Motivation 3
    Chapter Two: Organization Culture and Mission 9
    Chapter Three: Leadership Does Matter 21
    Chapter Four: Compensation Elements 31
    Chapter Five: You have Made Your Choice-Hit the Ground
    Running 37

Phase II: Performance and Skills Management 41
    Chapter Six: Performance Evaluation and Feedback 43
    Chapter Seven: Career Coaching 55
    Chapter Eight: Communication Skills 59

Phase III: Career Strategies 63
    Chapter Nine: Career Path Planning 65
    Chapter Ten: Career Development 73
    Chapter Eleven: Relationship Building 77
    Chapter Twelve: Career Changes 85
    Chapter Thirteen: Career Challenges and Opportunities 93
    Chapter Fourteen: The Dream of Business Ownership 101

Phase IV: Personal Brand and Behavior 107
    Chapter Fifteen: Defining Who You Are 109
    Chapter Sixteen: Change Agent and Being the Standard 113
    Chapter Seventeen: Ethics–Putting it All Together 117
    Chapter Eighteen: Professional Etiquette and Behavior 121

Career Assessments 129

Strategic Career Messages to Live By 133

Conclusion: Career Strategy Open Letter 139

Author's Note

I refuse to believe that there are people who wake up each day with the intention of doing a poor job and failing to make positive contributions to their chosen profession. There are no desirable payoffs from poor career performance and inappropriate behavior. Some individuals might be in the wrong profession, position or might not have the required skills to perform effectively but most people do want to perform and achieve personal goals. I have communicated this message to my employees, peers, and business associates for years. I emphasized this point during human resources planning discussions as a way of encouraging the development of all human assets. When that occurs, productivity improves, capital use is more efficient, organizations become more competitive and the overall standard of living ultimately improves—everyone wins.

I am very excited about writing this book because it gives me pleasure to share the many lessons learned about career management from over 30 years of business experience. Over time, I have learned what works and what does not work. I have certainly made some mistakes but learned a number of lessons. I did not have the value of what is now being sharing with you before I began my career but it is my pleasure to share my observations and wisdom. I encourage you to use this information as a tool for doing the things that will make your career more professionally rewarding and personally satisfying. Let us start with a few definitions from *"Webster"* to get everyone on the same page.

Successful \Suc*cess"ful\
Resulting in success; assuring, or promotive of, success; accomplishing what was proposed; having the desired effect; hence, prosperous; fortunate; happy; as, a successful use of medicine; a successful experiment; a successful enterprise.

Career \Ca*reer"\
General course of action or conduct in life, or in a particular part or calling in life, or in some special undertaking; usually applied to course or conduct which is of a public character; as, Washington's career as a soldier.

Management \Man"age*ment\ The act or art of managing; the manner of treating, directing, carrying on, or using, for a purpose; conduct; administration; guidance; control; as, the management of a family or of a farm; the management of state affairs.

Introduction

The road of success is like running up an escalator going down, you need to keep running, if you walk, you stand still, if you stop you are going down!

Anneloes Zuiderveen

Thirty years from now, you will regret more the things you did not do during your career than the things you did. Be one of the rare individuals who minimize those regrets by doing the necessary things to maximize your career success. I will take you on a journey that will outline the many things I would have improved or done differently during the selection process and management of my career. They are the many lessons learned that most individuals rarely get from formal education and training.

When I began this project, I felt that I would be sharing lots of technical and leadership information on the topic of career management. After all, I had done this for 33 years and had many answers. After a tremendous amount of research, reflection, and yes, soul searching, it became clear that the thing that makes some individuals successful, and others not, is behavior. Your behavior is a reflection of the things you do that lead to success. The more you practice and do the behavioral things I will discuss, the more successful you will be. Behavior is the bridge that separates the poor performers from average and average from commendable. That is why you see individuals with seemingly equal technical skills and aptitude achieving vastly different levels of career success. They manage their destiny by having goals and supporting them by taking action. They have the courage to follow their dreams.

Key behavioral traits lead to the necessary continuous learning and development of both technical and leadership skills required for success. The good news is that once you develop the traits, the technical and leadership activities become easier and more natural. You do the things required to be at the top of your profession. They become your values and your personal brand; how others identify you.

Several years ago, I had the opportunity to participate in a recruiting strategy session for a fortune 500 company. I was pleased to be able to do this because I firmly believe that organizations will be limiting their degree of success by the quality of their people. Yes, you must have a good product or service, and an implementation strategy but people are the way you get things done. This is the reason I have always believed in hiring the best people possible.

Dr. Jean Schelhorn, Research Laboratory Director, was asked to make a presentation at the beginning of the meeting to set the stage for the desired outcomes from the session. One of her introduction slides said, "If I could live my career over, I would..." I do not remember the total context and results of the meeting but I remember the introduction like it was yesterday. It really got my attention and made me think about the limited knowledge most individuals have about managing their careers in order to achieve maximum success. I thought about how most career strategies are learned through experience, done by trial and error, or learned when it was too late to be of value. Many of us seem to be content with going with the flow and believing someone else will manage our careers. NEVER believe someone else will have your best interest as his or her top priority. Career management is an individual responsibility.

For a bit of historical perspective, I was promoted three times in the first five years of my career and was one of the youngest department managers in the company at the age of 27. Promotions continued on a somewhat regular basis leading to increased levels of responsibility. At the time of this meeting, I had already held a number of executive finance positions for a fortune 500 company. By most standards, this level of achievement would be considered successful, both in terms of level in the organization, responsibility and compensation.

After a 33-year career in the business world, I personally know that my career processes should have been managed more effectively and the results could have been very different. At the beginning of my career, I did not know many of the written and unwritten rules needed in order to be successful in the corporate environment. Even worse, I was not aware of this deficiency. I did not have the information and knowledge required to bridge the gap between my good academic preparation and career success. An effective strategy could have been used that would have made the journey more pleasant, personally satisfying, and more successful. I would have dealt with many situations differently, been more able to control or anticipate actions and reactions, and been more prepared overall. I could have made improvements in a number of areas.

My sincere desire for this book is to share with you the wisdom I have gained over the years that will improve the way you manage and make career decisions. I know that my career accomplishments would have been even better if I had the benefit of the knowledge I am now sharing from my actual experience. I would have made better and more informed choices, performed at a higher level, corrected development areas sooner, focused more attention on critical success elements, continuously learned, and taken more calculated risks. I am confident your career accomplishments will be improved if you implement the strategies I am sharing. In the end, you will say that I told you the truth. Enjoy the journey.

Phase I: Career Selection and Decision Process

Chapter One:
Self-Assessment and Your Motivation

Hold fast to dreams, for if dreams die, life is a broken winged bird that cannot fly.

Langston Hughes

Your career selection is one of the most important things you will do in life. Considering the fact that you will spend a significant amount of your time in activities associated with your career, you should devote the necessary time to the process to make the most-informed decision possible. This is even more important now that many of us can virtually work from anywhere and at anytime due to the continuing expanded use of technology. You no longer leave everything behind at the end of the traditional workday. In addition to the work environment, we often develop life long personal relationships that affect other portions of our lives. That is natural because most of us develop relationships with people that we spend the most time. Many of our non-career related activities are the direct result of our career contacts. These associations strengthen the bond as ell as the need for a tension free and enjoyable work experience.

Many of our career selections are made without the benefit of a self-assessment to determine if we are motivated to do the responsibilities associated with that career. We simply select something we think we would like to do using self-developed criteria and limited supporting data. We do this with no real exposure to the responsibilities of the career or first hand knowledge of the likely positions in the career path. This is a much too important decision to make on blind faith. When doing my research, I wondered if this was the reason why a number of people interviewed were working in career areas that had no relationship to their initial area of education and training. Many had tried several careers and kept changing until they landed the career they found satisfying and rewarding. Some individuals lived with unsatisfying career choices and endured the pain of not following their dreams. Those individuals had significant things to say about reliving their careers. Many said they would make a number of changes to the decisions they had made the first time around. Some specifically said that not following their passion and dreams was their major career regret. Most were generally content with themselves in many ways but still wondered about the road not traveled. They had no way of knowing the outcome but knew that life would have been different had they followed their dreams and motivations.

Another approach for career selection is to use factual data that improves your odds of selecting a career that is consistent with your motivation. Motivational Appraisal of Personal Potential (MAPP) is now being used frequently as a tool for matching people with careers and professions. This appraisal does not determine whether you can or cannot perform in a job or career, but indicates if you will perform. It essentially determines the things that drive you from the inside, your *passion*. My experience and research indicates that people will learn required skills when they are motivated. You do not have to force it because they are doing what they like to do. When that happens, it ceases to be work, as many of us know it to be and becomes fun and enjoyable. This is important in your career selection because there will be bumps in the road and you need things that sustain you. When you are doing what you really enjoy, that is a major sustaining factor. If you have not taken one of the many motivational assessments, I suggest you do so no matter where you are in your career selection process or making other career choices. You need to know what really drives you; if you do not, you might miss real opportunities for career satisfaction.

Review the motivational assessment processes at www.assessment. com and you might discover some revealing information about what really drives you. You should also consider signing up for the newsletter on this site because it provides very useful strategic career information. There are other evaluations systems that work very well; this just happens to be one that I am familiar with and have personally taken. I found the results to be helpful for verifying and setting career goals. Doing so just might put you ahead of the process because these tools are being used in a number of businesses and industries as part of the human resources management process. They have been used for hiring, promoting, career planning, team assignments, succession planning, and outplacement processes. The evaluations are relatively quick to complete but provide an abundance of useful information. The results from the assessments have been positive.

Most of us are average. Most of us have average talents and abilities. I, like most people, believed that people who were labeled *"successful"* obviously must be exceptionally intelligent. I am convinced this is not true.

Many technically smart people will never experience the label of being successful. Two of the major things that separate the successful people from those who are not are their level of motivation and willingness to learn. When you are doing the things you are motivated to do; you have a built-in incentive to learn whatever is required to be the best at that endeavor. If you do not possess certain skills to accomplish your goals, motivation will drive you to obtain those skills.

Your passion and motivation will sustain you during those difficult times in your career. It is what will give you the energy to stay focused, even when it seems things are not going in the right direction. This reminds me of one of my most difficult, yet rewarding assignments during my corporate career. I became the finance leader of a major business that had been acquired three years prior to my joining the organization. Most people in the corporation felt that acquisition was a poor decision, and it was difficult attracting quality people to the organization. Each year after the acquisition, the business lost money. It was projected to lose another $60 million the same year I took control. Everything you could imagine was wrong with the business, costs were out of control, efficiencies were low, poor material quality, high labor costs, low market share, outdated equipment, and the list goes on.

I was very familiar with the organization and knew what had to happen in order to turn things around. I was acquainted with the person I would be interviewing with (as a matter-of-fact, we are still friends to this day). The interview was short and included a presentation he had recently given to the board of directors. Seeing as the business was loaded with issues, I felt I would be an asset to the business and deliver solutions. Apparently, he agreed and I was hired. Though the challenges seemed boundless, I was motivated to do what was necessary to make the required improvements. I liked working with people, solving problems, analyzing operations, evaluating financial data and investment options, and making decisions that affected results. I also liked variety and this position had an abundance of it. I would be working with numerous people, both internally and externally, as well as with multiple functions in 21 manufacturing facilities.

This business eventually attracted highly motivated individuals who enjoyed a challenge. The motivation, the skills, and positive attitude of this group resulted in a winning combination. Everyone knew that there would never be a day when we could say, *"mission accomplished."* We knew we could look forward to challenges as we strived to make continuous improvements but we were all willing to do what was necessary. The business made the needed changes and turned out to be a very profitable enterprise. Real friendships developed because everyone was in it together and willing to support required efforts. I know that everyone who took an assignment in that business improved his or her skills tremendously. Difficult assignments have that as a clear advantage over the easy, less challenging assignments. Do not be afraid to support your motivation by developing the required skills to get what you want from your career. Take those challenging assignments that will expand your skills. Doing the rewarding things that you have a passion for is career enhancing.

That experience occurred long ago and I recently received a message from an engineer I worked with during those days. I had not seen him for several years and he had gotten my contact information from a mutual acquaintance. He mentioned how much he missed the times we spent in that business. He also thanked me again for my support and for making difficult times fun and rewarding. Many of the people in that business were able to do and accomplish many of the things they were motivated to do and the hard work did not matter. The moral to this is that people generally enjoy challenging work and I am sure you are no exception. They also like rewarding work that they are motivated to do because it is their passion. This is what makes it fun and exciting. Settle for nothing less and you will really enjoy your career experiences. Strive to make your career choice have as many of those passion elements that sustain you as possible.

You can confirm your motivation with either internships or temporary assignments depending where you are in your career. Internships for high school, college, or vocational students are an excellent way to get a first hand feel for your likes and dislikes for the potential career path you are considering. For those of you who are currently employed but thinking of making a career change; consider temporary assignments as a way of evaluating possible career choices. You have everything to gain and nothing to loose with this approach and the quality of your career decision will improve. If you decide to target an internship or temporary assignment, do so with the same level of excitement and enthusiasm you would if you were in a permanent assignment. You must to do that in order to get a fair evaluation and assessment of what you can expect from the position and job responsibilities. These types of assignments can, and often do, lead to permanent placement. Another reason you need to take this type of proactive approach is because the organization will be looking at and evaluating you as well, and you do want to leave a positive impression no matter how the relationship turns out.

With any type of initial career arrangement, you will be building skills, learning and experiencing new things while expanding your network of contacts. All of these will strengthen your resume for future opportunities.

Those additional skills will make you even more valuable in the market. Expanding your network can open doors within the organization you are affiliated with and their external customers, vendors and clients. Anyone you meet can be a future resource for career opportunity. More people will get to know you and recognize your abilities. Should you avail yourself to this type opportunity, use it to maximum advantage.

No matter how sophisticated we get with defining our motivations and connecting people with careers, there still seems to be stress in the workplace. No one has figured out a way to eliminate it for a sustained period. I have never seen that happen and have never known anyone who has experienced that type of long-term, stress-free work environment. You do hear a lot about stress management programs, employee assistance programs, and the desire for a more balanced life. I see no sign of a slower-paced and less stressful work environment. If anything, logic would tell us that in our fast-paced and ever-changing world, life changes would become even more fast-paced and volatile in the future. Life cycles on businesses, products, services, processes, and yes, careers are shorter and all of those things bring about anxiety and potential stress

Recognizing this, you need to identify those things that sustain you over time. Those are the supports and influences that are important to you and will be with you for a lifetime. We often hear that faith, family, and friends are the things that sustain us. This is personal and you must make your own determination. Do that because you will certainly need to know. The things that sustain you provide critically needed comfort and support. It is the support you need when things are not as you desire and you are experiencing anxiety. These are the times when you need someone just to talk to and not for specific work-related advice. You need this comfort when you encounter the difficult manager, peers, customer, or assignment, and you cannot find the needed focus or solution. Your sustaining forces will be your soft place to land for those bumps in the road during your career. You will need them no matter how well you are motivated to do what you have chosen to do or how great your aptitude is for your chosen career field.

Chapter Two:
Organization Culture and Mission

Far better it is to dare mighty things, to win glorious triumphs even though checkered by failure, than to rank with those poor spirits who neither enjoy nor suffer much because they live in the gray twilight that know neither victory nor defeat.

Theodore Roosevelt

I will discuss organizational culture rather extensively because it is likely the main facilitators of everything an organization does or fails to do. Culture drives the major elements that influence the ultimate performance and results that any organization delivers in its activities. Culture will be a factor in many of your defining moments during your career. Think about the organizations you personally know and how their *"personalities"* have evolved over time. The culture is established because leaders attempt to surround themselves with people who generally think and act the way they prefer. I will also discuss ways of recognizing and adjusting to changes in an organization's culture. I have been amazed at how quickly organizations can take on the personality of its leadership. Be very sensitive to culture when making your career choices, it will influence both your and the organization's degree of success.

Culture is sometimes thought of as intangible –not something that you can see or easily identify. This is not true; there are specific traits that will give you a relatively good understanding of an organization's culture. They will not necessarily be clear and visible at all times, but you will be able to see the trends. Let us look at a few items that can give you an indication of an organization's culture. Some areas will vary depending on the type of business, organization, or service involved but many will be common no matter what type organization. Consider the following elements of organizational culture when evaluating your potential career affiliations.

1. **Values:** The values of the organization must reflect virtue and be understood by everyone. Are they consistent in all parts of the organization? Do the values clearly communicate the need to operate with the highest degree of honesty and integrity?

2. **Customer:** No matter what your profession, you must have customers. The organization must recognize that the market place and customers drive everything it does. Are the policies, procedures, and practices of how the organization treats customers clear? Is the organization responsive to customer needs and concerns? Are there measurements that indicate the level of customer satisfaction?

3. **Technology:** Is there a strong and developing sense of the importance of technology in the organization? How does the technology literacy in the organization compare to its competition? Will the current and/or planned technology allow the organization to compete relative to cost performance and productivity? Is the organization a leader in technology, fast follower, or lagging?

4. **Measurement of success:** In order to get better at what you are doing, you must continuously measure your results because you get results on the things you measure. Does everyone in the organization understand the measurement of success? Does the organization have the right measures and key drivers defined and well understood by all? Are indicators such as customer satisfaction and shareholder value being used as measures? Are measures such as month-to-month or quarter-to-quarter improvements being used to insure continuous improvement and are they communicated to all stakeholders?

5. **Decision-making:** In a rapid changing environment, it is essential that productive organizations operate with a well-defined level of authority and minimum bureaucracy. Speed is essential for success. Is decision making responsibility delegated at the appropriate level? Is there an entrepreneurial spirit that facilitates speed and responsiveness to changing events? Do the people feel and act empowered?

6. **Planning:** Look for planning patterns over time in order to determine how well the organization understands and manages its businesses. Is the organization operating with a clear strategic vision supported by operating tactics? Has the planning processes

delivered consistent results? Have the business plans been completed with quality or have they required frequent major adjustments?

7. **Continuous learning:** Continuous learning is critical for your personal growth; it keeps your skills contemporary. You need to keep this as a priority in order to make sure you can continue to deliver value in your chosen profession. You should also look at the statistics of number of promotions from within as a barometer of how effective the learning and development process has been in the past. Is this an organization known for being progressive and believing that it is necessary to continue the development process by supporting internal and external training and development programs? Are employees given challenging assignments that allow for growth and development? Are the people in the organization allowed to innovate and try new things in order to utilize the full scope of their skills?

8. **Change:** Is this an organization that has a culture of recognizing the importance of change in order to deliver continuing improved value? Is the importance of changing before being forced to by the competition valued and supported? Has the organization demonstrated the ability to change in the past with successful outcomes?

9. **Quality of people:** A content and well-motivated workforce might be the best indicator you can find of the total effectiveness of an organization's culture. When the people are satisfied and content, the organization is doing many of the right things. If the organization has an ineffective, negative culture, the people will not be satisfied and you are likely to see significant turnover. Good people will not stay with an organization that has a culture that is not working. Does the organization have a reputation for attracting, developing, retaining, and promoting people from within? Is the organization a preferred place of employment? Do the people like the work they are doing and their overall work environment?

10. **Community:** Organizations must give back to the local communities in order to be valued as good citizens. This can affect employee moral as well as the organization's ability to have community support when needed. Is the organization sensitive to and responsive to community needs? Does it share and give back to communities in positive ways? Are employees openly encouraged to participate in community-related activities and projects?

Culture is the foundation of all organizations guiding principles. That is the case if you are operating as a soul proprietorship or part of a large organization. Good organizations feel pride in its culture and want these principles communicated and well understood by the internal organization as well as the outside public. The practice of letting others know what you stand for can aid in achieving the organization's goals. Organizations also use it as a recruiting tool to attract people who share the same values. Organizations get better when it has motivated people with a shared vision and values. Strive to be or affiliate with an organization that has a culture of establishing defined goals, measures results, instills an entrepreneurial spirit, delegates effectively, and treats people with individual dignity. Value these principles when making your career choices and decisions; they will be important to your success.

The culture of organizations can and must change during the course of its existence. There will come a time during the life cycle of any business enterprise or profession when you must change dramatically in order to move to the next level. If the moment is missed and you fail to recognize the need to do things differently, the organization will begin to decline. No organization can stay the same perpetually. Either it will change on its terms or their competition will force it to change. That is the nature of a free enterprise system.

It is possible to recognize when an organizational cultural change is occurring and the change can occur much quicker than believed possible. Significant, radical change rarely occurs from within any organization. It does not happen because organizations, just like individuals, have a comfort zone. It is the place where everyone is comfortable and like things just as they have been for years. The feelings are that things have been good for a very long time so why fix what is not broken. Most will have a tendency to believe that if the organization continues doing what it has the very worse scenario is that results will either stay the same or get marginally better. It is rather easy to understand this type of sentiment. That is the comfortable way of thinking but it is not true. Organizations and individuals like the things they create and believe the results are just fine. They believe it is the only way things should be done.

I personally witnessed an organizational cultural change that affected about 18,000 employees. I admit that many of the employees who had been with the organization for a number of years were somewhat resistant to change. They knew all the things that had been tried over the years and felt that they knew what would and would not work. They knew their contributions and those of others whom they respected and felt comfortable with their work over the years. They forgot that it was a different time and different situations existed. Change is constant and nothing stays the same. It took me a while to realize that some things done in the past were not the only, or necessarily the best, alternative. I got to this point by thinking about how the markets, competition, and technologies had changed. I also realized that the organization was not making any real forward progress and had actually begun to decline. It was clear to me that a significant change in culture was required to make progress.

A leadership change at the top of an organization is likely the most effective way to change an organization drastically. It is also the way to change quickly. I experienced the change and it was both quick and significant. When a new individual joins an organization at the top, they often like to surround themselves with people that make them feel comfortable. In many instances, they are different people than those supported by the previous organization. That is when you are likely to see the cultural change begin. Think about it, they already had a comfort zone and it is certainly one that is different from the one in the existing organization. It does not mean that all of the ideas and approaches of the new people are superior and clearly better but they will be different.

One of the first things you will see is a number of new people joining the organization. The new leadership will need people in order to make the change process effective. They need loyal people; furthermore, individuals who share the same ideas and goals as the new leadership. Watch what the new people say and do to observe the changes or differences in the operating philosophy of the organization. We are all a product of our experiences so we simply do what we have always done. The new leadership team that enters will bring their biases, just different from the past. Once you observe the new people and see what they do, you will begin to see the new culture emerge.

A new mission statement and guiding principles are likely communication vehicles to help facilitate the desired change. This puts information in the hands of everyone in the organization to minimize confusion in future direction. The mission statements and guiding principles I have reviewed are normally simple, concise and very easy to understand. They leave very little room for personal interpretation. Organizations will communicate the mission and principles frequently. I have seen the guiding principles included on the back of business cards and on stationary. They will be supported by specific actions to let the new culture begin to emerge.

Next, look for major changes in processes that really begin to make a difference. The policies and procedures facilitate the consistency needed until the new actions become natural. They begin to take life after they have been repeated for some time and this formalizes that things are different from the past. They become the new ways of doing things and part of the new culture.

We have all heard the statement that people are an organizations most important asset. I really believe this is true. When organizational cultural change is occurring, you are likely to see changes in recruiting practices. The organization will be looking to hire new people with skills, abilities, and philosophies compatible with the new mission and culture. This will be the case for new hires, experienced placements, and promotions from within the organization. Investigate new opportunities that fit your skills and talents; you might find the changes personally rewarding.

You will begin to see some relatively high level individuals from the prior administration leave the organization that is now under new leadership. The public announcements are likely to read as follows.

I regretfully report that Mr. John Doe has decided to leave our company to pursue other career opportunities. We sincerely thank John for his many years of productive service and valuable contributions. We will all certainly miss his impact. We wish John and his family the very best in their future endeavors.

There are other statements in organizational announcements that do not actually say it but really mean, *"You're fired."* Look for statements such as:

- He/she will be leaving to pursue other career interest.
- He/she will be leaving to spend more time with family.
- He/she will be leaving to take advantage of new career opportunities.
- He/she will be leaving for personal reasons.

The announcements will never be specific or anticipated by the general employment population. In addition, the individuals being affected will likely leave quickly. I have actually seen the person being terminated out of the office before the announcement is published. Do not count on being invited to a going away celebration; that will not happen. The real meaning of the announcement is that this individual did not agree with the new organization's culture and the changes that will be occurring. The agreement was that the individual could not function and work in the new environment. This does not necessarily mean that one individual was right and the other wrong. It simply means their positions and philosophies were different and incompatible. Sometimes changes or adjustments are required in order to avoid conflicts and disruptions within organizations.

Each individual in the organization will be required to make some decisions. The first one will be to decide if you really embrace the new culture, vision, and guiding principles. If you do, you have a chance to function in the new organization. The next element, or hurdle, will test your compatibility with the new people that are entering the organization. Their personalities, technical, and leadership skills and abilities are the most likely areas to be significantly different. You must have a reasonable comfort level with them to function effectively. Finally, you need to be comfortable with the new operating philosophy, policies, and procedures and yes, the unwritten rules

If faced with this type of organizational cultural change, my advice is to give the new organization a legitimate chance by keeping an open mind. Change can be very positive and good for an organization as well as the individuals involved. Do not leave in haste just because you are being asked to think and act differently. Do not let your comfort zone ruin a potentially good career. After all, the new organization can be a new career start for you that might be very exciting. You just might find that you have opportunities you never thought possible. Take the time to evaluate the total situation and develop your personal operating strategy. You are really in a good position of strength because you know a lot about the organization and can contribute. It is very possible that you can really thrive in the organization with new leadership.

If after giving the new leadership and organization a fair chance, you determine that you are not happy and cannot function professionally, you owe it to yourself to make a change. Make your change, but do it right. Leave on the best of terms possible and do not burn bridges. Make an effort to leave the door open; the grass might not be greener on the other side. I have seen individuals leave organizations but return later, often to a much better position.

There are other types of organizational changes that are more significant than a leadership change at the top. This can be the case irrespective of how complete your assessment of the organization was relative to its overall strength and how it has performed in the past. Market forces can be strong enough to force changes that were never conceived during planning processes. The changes could be in the form of restructuring, mergers, or acquisitions. The organization could be the one taking the action or the victim of an action by an outside organization. In either situation, the changes are likely to be significant and will happen quickly. These types of changes or business combinations are normally driven by the belief that shareholder value will be improved. This typically means that the focus will be on leveraging resources, reducing costs, gaining market share, improving productivity, bottom line profitability, or some combination of these and other less tangible factors.

The bottom line is that things will be much different and quickly. In a rapidly changing or growing industry, it is not unusual to see an organization experience multiple combinations within a few years. This can be traumatic to some in the organization who are not capable of dealing with rapid change and confusion. There are likely to be changes in processes, procedures, approvals for actions and major system changes in technology. The new phrases you are likely to hear are *change, adapt to change,* and *understand the new rules.*

The best way to adjust during change situations is to do as more listening than talking. Observe what is happening and get involved by contributing to the process. Understand the new rules as best you can as quickly as possible. Good, competent organizations recognize the amount of anxiety business integrations can cause and they focus on communicating frequently and with as much specific detail as possible. They realize that the worse thing that can happen to an organization is to allow the rumor mill to take control of the communication process. If you are at the leadership level, communicate the facts. If you are not at the leadership level, and do not have facts, do not participate in the rumor mill. Listen and react to the facts as communicated. These type situations can be winning scenarios for all involved. The organization wants to be successful and will need the support of the people to accomplish their goals. In many ways, this can be a new start, so approach it as a way to kick starting your career for maximum potential. You have a new chance to make a first impression.

As you analyze your various options for your career choice, make sure you balance the organization's culture with your personal values. You know yourself better than anyone and certainly know the areas where you cannot or will not compromise. You know your likes, dislikes, and things you find rewarding and the things that go against your basic values. Never put yourself in a compromising situation; you will not be content or able to do your best work.

I hope that you have researched the organization and have reasonable knowledge regarding the organization's culture, guiding principles, mission, and operating objectives. These are the key elements that define an organization. Organizations are in many ways just like individuals in that characteristics, traits, and actions define who the organization is and what it does. These elements guide the actions taken internally and externally. It defines how the organization treats its employees, associates, suppliers, and customers.

It is critical that you compare your beliefs and values to those of the organization that you are affiliated with or are considering. Do this as quantitatively as possible to make sure there are no major gaps that will make you uncomfortable. As an example, if you are very environmentally sensitive, you do not want to join a company or organization that has no respect for the environment. The only exception to this would be in a case where the organization has recognized issues of the past and is actively working to change. In that case, your potential impact could be extremely rewarding, as you very well could be an impact contributor. A negative situation could become a positive experience.

Organizations establish their cultural identity for a number of reasons. Culture sets the stage for the vision, mission, strategic plans, operating plans, and implementing strategies. There should be published documents for each of these that communicate what the current expectations are in order to deliver the planned outcomes. These are the key initiatives that drive organizations to goal accomplishment. The people responsible for getting the job done must be aware of all relevant expectations. Review the details of each of these strategies with the objective of gaining a good understanding of how you can deliver value to the essential processes.

Do not stop with just reviewing the plans, review actual performance to see how the organization has delivered on their plans. Review to determine if the current culture has translated into business or services success. For public traded companies, complete *"due diligence"* level research by looking at 10K reports, proxies, recent business announcements, and annual reports. Look to see if the organization is a leader in their market as measured by placement versus competition. Top performers in a given business segment will likely be number one or two in their businesses. Some businesses can be successful as niche competitors but that must be a well-defined strategy that is understood by everyone in the organization. This type review and analysis will result in you making a more informed decision regarding your career choices.

Be aware that not all potentially successful businesses will have a proven record of accomplishment that you can look at and actually see in audited financial statements. In this age of rapid change and innovation, new industries will be starting up while others will be going away. You will serve yourself well to take your blinders of for start up opportunities and new ventures that could prove to be of value to your career success. New ventures can be extremely exciting, learning opportunities, and financially rewarding. Just think about the individuals who got involved with firms like Microsoft, Wal-Mart, Dell, PeopleSoft, and many other start-up firms in the past. None of them had long-term, proven records of accomplishment but turned out to be extremely successful and rewarding both professionally and financially for those who got involved with the new ventures.

Organizational culture will be a significant factor in the degree of satisfaction you will get from any organization. Review the organization you are affiliated with or considering joining to see if the current culture has driven it to a sustainable competitive advantage. That is the true long-term measure of success, which the culture has delivered. If the culture is not right for you, you will have a job and not a career. You will not be able to become the very best you can be when being affiliated with an organization which has a culture that is not compatible with your core beliefs.

When evaluating an organization's culture, you will find it beneficial to get a clear understanding of its mission. Organizations of all sizes need to have a defined mission that is communicated. The mission statement is not just for internal use, it should be shared with all stakeholders; including customers, shareholders, suppliers, contractors, employees, and consultants. Anyone who can influence the organization's results needs to know and understand the mission. Brevity is encouraged with these statements with the intent being a concise and easily understood message. The key elements of mission statements are:

- Brief description of what the organization does
- Vision of what the organization wants to become
- Philosophies and values that will characterize actions
- Key strategies for reaching goals
- What distinguishes the organization from its competitors

Reviewing the mission statement will give you an understanding of how the culture has translated into a clear vision for the future. Some mission statements are very simple but effective when supported by strong strategic and operating plans. A simple but effective mission statement is the one for Google. Google's is to organize the world's information and make it universally accessible and useful. This statement leaves room for a significant amount of innovation and creativity on the part of those involved in implementation of business strategies. It has proven to be very successful for that organization and has translated into significant shareholder value. It is certainly supported by strong tactics and leadership with clear accountability for delivering results.

General Electric uses a broad vision statement or tagline to establish its culture. At General Electric, the tagline is *"we bring good things to life."* This vision facilitates the company's mission, strategies and operating tactics creating, dozens of profitable businesses. The organization has broken down barriers between the internal organizations allowing a free flow of information and solutions between its leadership and all employees. The workforce is empowered to act decisively and sees the value of continuous learning as a vehicle for productivity improvement. Town hall meetings called Work-Out support this culture: meetings designed to encourage employee feedback, cross-pollination of ideas and employee empowerment.

The mission statements are likely to be public knowledge; however, the strategic and operations plans are proprietary and confidential. Organizations typically will reserve this information for individuals responsible for influencing the results. Those on the outside of an organization will not be able to review this level of detail. You might be able to get some general understanding of how you might be expected to affect some of the strategies before joining the organization but that is about it. You also must be aware that the mission of organizations can and do evolve over time. Change is required in order to stay relevant. The more you understand about the organization's mission and culture, the better prepared you will be to perform and add value. This understanding can be the foundation for a successful career as it gives you what you need in order to be more focused on the important goals.

Chapter Three:
Leadership Does Matter

Good leaders make people feel that they're at the very heart of things, not at the periphery. Everyone feels that he or she makes a difference to the success of the organization. When that happens people feel centered and that gives their work meaning.

Warren Bennis

Leadership is defined by *"Webster"* as the position or office of an authority figure. Leaders are seen as influential people with the ultimate responsibility for delivering results. Some leadership positions are elected, some appointed, and sometimes by an agreed succession plan. You will sometimes see individuals in leadership positions with no one being able to understand how the individual became a leader. Some individuals get good leadership positions without paying any of the typical dues necessary for the accomplishment. In all honesty, some promotions occur without logic or reasons that are understood. Favors do happen and that is the way it is; so do not get overly upset when it happens in the organization you are affiliated with. While this is unfortunate, it is life in a capitalistic system and one of the rules of the game you will not see published very often. No, the playing field is not always level and that is something you will likely have to deal with at some point during your career.

Leaders can have varying degrees of effectiveness depending on style, preparation, knowledge of the required processes, motivation, and attitude. You are likely to experience multiple types of leaders during your career. When selecting your organization affiliation or while managing your career, you should pay attention to the leadership qualities and performance of key leaders in the organization. There are different leadership styles, and those styles will affect your performance and how you are perceived internally and external to your organization. It will not only play a roll in what you do but also how you get things done. This will certainly affect your career satisfaction, and ultimately, your accomplishments. I have worked with and reported to individuals with a number of different styles and the differences can be significant. You will need to understand the styles and possibly learn to adapt to different approaches. Be assured that no two will be the same, some you will like, and others you will dislike. Learn not to take any of the situations personally; work on being effective.

You will find that some leaders will try to get things done by intimidation and brut force. Some will show little sensitivity and personal respect while others will be compassionate and very respectful. I always felt that overly demanding and intimidating leaders were somewhat self-centered and lacked confidence. Some leaders are just not very comfortable with themselves and flexible. Experience has taught me that this type personality will never develop a high performing sustainable organization. If you are someone who is a self-starter, aggressive, take charge individual and can function with little direction, I would suggest you avoid this type leader, if possible. You are likely to clash frequently and your time associated with this individual will not be pleasant. If it happens during your career and you feel that the situation will be temporary, develop strategies to manage the situation. That is possible and you might find it to be a character builder. We sometimes need different experiences in order to learn what not to do and who not to imitate later in our careers. Experiences are only a loss when you learn nothing.

I reject the intimidating leadership style and prefer a much different style that reflects respect and individual dignity. It is a style I enjoyed as a subordinate and one that I adopted as a leader. This style is one designed to unite the organization around a shared vision based on short and long-term goals. It also shows respect for the individual, allows for creativity, development, and supports self-esteem. It encourages innovation and initiative. It facilitates change and I see this as transformational leadership. This type leadership allows organizations to grow and mature to the point where they can function well when leadership changes or is away for extended periods. This style also nurtures future leaders by giving earned responsibility and the latitude to make decisions.

Another leadership trait you should consider when doing your evaluation is how the organization responds in difficult times. This is the real test for the quality of the leadership. Weak leaders are the ones who avoid, deny, delay, and ultimately spin the truth. You want to be affiliated with an organization that is known for having the highest ethical principles. That will be the type organization that has good long-term potential. One poor decision can put an organization on a path from which it can never recover; it is just that easy. One poor decision might not seem significant, but it can set the trend for future actions.

The number one reason why people leave or dislike their jobs is their boss. Leaders should have qualities supportive of development and personal growth. Below are the essential qualities managers or leaders should possess. These traits can also be looked upon as things good leaders must possess in order to sustain themselves long term. Be mindful of these leadership traits in order to improve your odds of having a pleasant and rewarding career experience.

1. **Consistency and fair treatment:** You want a leader who is decisive, consistent, and predictable. This allows you to anticipate actions and reactions without having constant direction. Inconsistent managers will eventually do or say something that will potentially cause confusion and possible conflict. You also want a manager who does not show partiality and treats everyone in the organization equally.

2. **Delegates effectively:** Ambitious employees want a manager who gives them quality assignments that supports their personal growth. These assignments allow for creativity and innovation while being exposed to new and challenging projects. In addition, these managers are open to new ideas and concepts while not believing their way is the only way.

3. **Frequent communicator:** You do not want an absentee manager who only shows up for a crisis. You want a manager that talks to you frequently and provides timely quality feedback on your projects and performance. You never want a manager who waits until your annual performance appraisal to advise you of a dated issue. That approach is not good for you or the organization.

4. **Honesty and Integrity:** This is a non-negotiable trait. A manager that does not possess this essential trait will be a continuing problem as long as he or she continues in a leadership position. Problems in this area can and often are career ending.

5. **Knowledgeable and technically competent:** Leaders and other employees' respect and support managers who are technically competent. These managers and their staffs are valued and appreciated in the organization.

6. **Decisive:** Managers who are decisive address organizational issues when they surface and do not avoid the tough decisions. They treat employee performance issues with sincere urgency and do

not allow them to negatively affect the morale of the organization. Managers who demonstrate this trait earn the respect of their peers as well as employees. Delaying decisions that are obvious helps no one.

7. **Recognizes excellence:** My survey results indicate that high performing, successful individuals like and appreciate being recognized for the results they achieve. Good manages understand this need and use various recognition techniques as motivational tools. When you feel appreciated, you will have incentive to contribute even more.

8. **Supports employees:** Employees want and respect leaders who will support them when issues with others in the organization arise. They want to know that they will not be left to stand alone to defend their positions when they are correct but unpopular with others.

9. **Innovator and embraces change:** Leaders who constantly innovate while embracing change get the attention of all in the organization and are valued. When the leader is valued, the organization they manage is valued and is looked to for guidance and solutions. You want to be affiliated with leaders and organizations that are valued.

10. **Interpersonal skills:** You do not necessarily have to socialize with the managers or leaders you work with but that individual should possess good interpersonal skills in order to make your work environment pleasant and enjoyable. Poor interpersonal skills create significant tension and you will not perform at your best if stressed and uncomfortable with your leader.

Given the amount of time you are likely to spend in the presence of this individual, you need to make sure you are comfortable with their philosophies, style, and actions. It needs to be someone who listens and responds to your needs. During your evaluation of organizations, observe how the management treats people. You want an organization that will support your personal and professional growth. Those organizations hire and promote leaders who can delegate effectively without losing control. I personally did my best learning while having the freedom to innovate. It was much more rewarding to have new and rewarding experiences. You do not want to be or work for a manager who has the philosophy that his or her way is the only way things should be done. That is a sure formula for long-term mediocrity and a complacent organization. That is an organization for gatekeepers and not progressive, innovative individuals. Staying the same is a sure path to burnout and boredom.

Remember that dissatisfaction with the boss is the number one reason why people leave their positions. Do your homework to support your organization and career affiliation decision. You need to understand what you will be getting just as the organization must have a feel for you and your capabilities. Always remember that all situations, including leaders or managers, are temporary and will change. If your manager has poor leadership skills, that deficiency at some point will be recognized. If you decide to join an organization while knowing there are some things you do not personally like about the current leadership, you might have to face a defining moment. If things do not work out to your satisfaction, you always have choices, and you might have to make a change. Before doing that, remember that all things will change and often quicker than anticipated.

Information sharing, also called a job interview, is needed and a valuable element to your career selection process. The typical interview is structured in a format where the potential employer will get what they feel is the required information needed to make a decision about you. You will be asked questions with the idea of evaluating your responses in order to determine if you are acceptable for the available position. Your career selection is much more than an individual being evaluated to determine if they will be acceptable to an organization. You also need information to determine if you will be getting what you need and want from the relationship. That is the only way the relationship will be long term and mutually beneficial. Let us look at what each party is likely to want to know about the other in order to achieve the desired relationship. Following are the things organizations will want from potential employees, or someone looking to affiliated with it in some capacity:

1. The organization will want you to be technically competent in the target position. They will also want to know if the individual will be motivated and passionate enough to perform at a sustained high level.
2. You will need to demonstrate that you have a positive attitude and will fit well within the organization. You must show that you have the ability to adjust and work with individuals with different personalities and levels of expertise in order to achieve results.
3. The organization will want to know if you will be an innovator, and not a gatekeeper. You must show that you recognize that things change and require continuous learning to deliver value.

4. Organizations look for and want self-starters who grow continuously, both personally and professionally. They will want to know if you will take initiative rather than waiting for your manager or leader to give or force-feed you the next assignment or project.

5. You will need to show that you have leadership qualities and good long-term potential. The organization will be investing a lot in you and are looking for someone who will advance in the organization. You will need to deliver long-term value in order to generate a return on their investment.

6. You must show that you are self-confident by your demonstrated record of accomplishment. Use positive terms when discussing what you would do in the organization given the opportunity to perform. Speak with enthusiasm and confidence about your abilities.

7. You must show that you posses good social skills and will project a positive image of the company, or organization. You will be representing the organization and how you act in various professional and social situations is a reflection of the organization as a whole and not just you personally.

8. You will need to show that you believe in and operate with the highest degree of honesty and integrity. Quality organizations want people they can trust to do the right thing at all times.

9. The hiring organization will want to know if you will be dependable and can be counted on to deliver quality results. Do what you said you would on time and with quality.

10. You must demonstrate good etiquette in order to thrive in any quality organization. Use these skills in every situation or encounter you have with your current or target organizations. In fact, always use these skills and let them become your natural self.

The interaction you have will go a long way toward sealing your fate with your current organization or the one you have targeted for a professional opportunity. You want to leave your targeted interviews with everyone you encounter feeling that you are a no lose candidate and a fit must be found for you in the organization. That is just how excited you want the decision makers to feel about you as an individual. Additionally, there are things you need to know about the organization you are evaluating. The objective is to have a mutually beneficial relationship that results in you also getting what you want from the relationship. The key things you want to have from the relationship are as follows:

1. Be confident that you will be motivated and passionate about the position in the organization and that the job content will have you doing the things you really like.
2. You need to feel that you will enjoy working for the manager of the organization for which you will be a direct report. Keep in mind that the boss is the number one reason people leave jobs so there must be a good fit in order for you to be comfortable.
3. Strong performers need and want to be challenged and you need to feel that the position will provide a challenge now and in the future.
4. Professionals need personal growth and the ability to innovate. Make sure you will be able to not only use your current talents but also have room for future growth. You will also need to know if you will be allowed to expand the position by taking on new and innovative responsibilities.
5. You need to be comfortable that there will be opportunities for continuous learning both internally and by way of external training and development from various outside sources. You will want to keep pace with or be ahead of your professional competition. Be able to say with confidence that continuous learning is a priority for the organization.
6. Make sure you will be treated and judged fairly relative to your peers in the organization. You will want to feel that you will get fair consideration for all available promotions in your immediate organization as well as in other parts of the organization for career broadening opportunities.
7. You will need to make sure you are comfortable with the placement of this specific business or organization within the industry that it participates. Make sure you feel that the business strategies will keep the organization competitive in its market or service area.
8. Evaluate to make sure others in the organization are respected for what they do and that they are treated with dignity and respect.
9. While no one in my survey mentioned money as an issue when discussing his or her career satisfaction, everyone wants to be fairly compensated and financially rewarded for his or her work. Make sure that your compensation is competitive and that it satisfies your personal needs.

Positive responses to the key items for both parties will result in mutually beneficial relationship. You can get the information you need by asking the right questions during each phase of the evaluation process. You will be talking with individuals who are knowledgeable about the organization being considered and they have data that you will not find in published documents. Most will be willing to share what they know, even more than they normally plan to. Advanced preparation will allow you to ask and answer all the questions needed to make an informed decision. Think about what you want to know in advance by writing them down and do not be caught cold with nothing to say.

You should also practice how you plan to respond to questions asked during the interview or information exchange session. Think about the commonly asked questions and be ready to show your strengths. Focus on how you will be able to add value to the organization by giving as many specific examples of your talents and capabilities as possible. If you are experienced at this point in your career, plan to talk in specific terms about what you have accomplished in prior positions. Never reveal proprietary or confidential information about a previous employer. If you will talk openly about that organization, the assumption will be made that you will do the same with this organization. Be truthful in all your responses; dishonesty is the one problem that is nearly impossible to recover from.

Your listening skills should be fine-tuned during your interview. You need to hear and understand specifically what the person is asking in order to respond correctly. If the question was not clear, politely ask for clarity in order to make sure your response is appropriate. One of the worse turn-offs during an interview is the feeling that the candidate does not have a clue about what is being discussed. It is easy to get the impression that the person is not competent. I know that is the impression I was left with when interviewing candidates. After thinking about it, I am sure that in some situations, the inappropriate answer might have been the result of a simple misunderstanding that was not cleared up.

Use your discussion time to make a positive impact and get information you need to make an informed decision. If you have a genuine interest in the organization, use this opportunity to use any hooks you might have in your arsenal. Keep this in mind while doing your research about the organization and make a note about all potential connections. Search the internet and read biographies of the key executives. Find out where they have worked during their careers. Where did they attend school? Have they lived in your city or town at any point? Do you have any friends or relatives currently working for the organization? Are you a member of any affiliated industry organizations? Do you possess any non-conflict or interest client, competitor, or vendor linkage that is of value? Specific career, industry, or personal hooks can be keys to you being the preferred candidate for the available position. Use your hooks to aid you at the appropriate stages in the selection process. Weave them into the conversation and never make it intimidating to the interviewer. Look at them only as a competitive advantage.

Chapter Four:
Compensation Elements

If you want to succeed, you should strike out on new paths, rather than travel the worn paths of accepted success.

John D Rockefeller

Your compensation will not and should not be the single motivating factor for your career choices. Compensation alone will not sustain you during a long-term career. It has not been my main motivator over the years and was not for those successful individuals I surveyed while doing my research for this book. Several individuals did indicate the need to be valued and fairly compensated for what they did and that should be your expectation as well. They also talked about the need to have an understanding about the earning potential for career choices. You do require a certain level of compensation to support your needs, so why not find ways to be compensated while following your passion.

Compensation occurs in a number of forms and the more you understand about the system and process; the more equipped you will be to influence your level of compensation. You should never leave the process exclusively to others to understand and manage while trusting that you will always be treated fairly. That does not always happen because organizations generally try to minimize costs and maximize profits. They want maximum value for all cash out-flow. I have personally worked in and managed organizations with several individuals having essentially the same position description and job title but different compensation. The reasons for this might be supportable but you must understand the rules in order to insure you are being treated fairly. Organizations can use compensation as a tool for attracting, retaining, and motivating employees and affiliates. It is generally one of the first things most of us consider when making our initial career choice. We see this as a message regarding how we are valued by the organization.

Compensation is much more than what you are paid weekly, biweekly, monthly, or annually. As recognition of this, many organizations have converted to a total rewards system that is communicated to employees and affiliates. The system attempts to recognize the value of all cash, non-cash, and intangible forms of compensation and benefits. Organizations use their complete package of potential rewards to attract and retain the people they want and value. You will want to evaluate the total rewards package you will be receiving when doing your evaluation while making your career choice. Being well-informed is one of the ways you can potentially avoid resentment in the future because of not having a complete understanding of your total compensation. Good knowledge of all compensation elements will enable you to negotiate your best package initially and manage the process in the future. Focus on getting an understanding of the following elements of compensation:

1. **Base salary:** This reflects the cash wages paid to an employee, normally on a weekly, bi-weekly, or monthly basis. The primary work forces are normally paid weekly based on an hourly rate that is established by the organization management or a negotiated rate for employees represented by a collective bargaining agreement. Professionals are generally compensated bi-weekly or monthly based on an assigned rating for the specific position involved. This is based on a value assigned to the position and is supported by an evaluation of the value impact to the organization. Comparisons are made to comparable positions in the industry or field of endeavor. The actual pay amount can, and often does, vary by individual based on qualifications, experience, performance, tenure, and long term potential. Business owners have access to retained earning, the net after tax income that remains after all other expenses have been paid. Decisions will then be made for the level of personal compensation versus reinvestment in the business.

2. **Commission compensation:** This is potentially the most variable form of compensation as it is driven by direct acts of the individual. Some positions have a combination of base salary and commissions with varying percentages of total compensation base on specific actions or results. You are more likely to see this form of compensation in areas such as sales or manufacturers representatives. In many ways, you can look at this the same as

you would the idea of investing (i.e. more risk but the potential compensation can be much greater).

3. **Bonus or incentive compensation:** This is compensation reflective of a bonus paid for achieving specified performance objectives. For best results, the objectives are communicated well in advance in order to get the desired improved performance. This form can be used for the base job, a special target situation needing change, or for both.

4. **Stock options:** This compensation comes in the form of specific stock grants or options to buy a specific quantity of stock in the business at a specified price for a given time period. Stock options can, and are being used for both start-up as well as established organizations. They, at one time, were reserved for the elite but have become more common for other levels of employees, contractors, or consultants. The reasons for using this form of compensation vary but the organization wants something specific from the individual or group of individuals involved.

5. **Sign-on bonus**: These are no longer exclusively for the high paid athlete or top executives. Sing-on bonuses are now being paid to individuals at various levels in organizations. You can be assured that they will be restricted to those individuals who are perceived to have real measurable value and not just average capability and worth.

6. **Indirect compensation:** This form of compensation includes items typically classified as benefits. These items are not cash in hand, but they do have significant value and must be considered when evaluating total compensation levels. Many organizations have a flexible benefits structure, which allows individual employees to select the benefits they need, or desire, based on personal choice. Some typical benefits are health insurance, life insurance, flexible spending accounts, 401K plan, childcare assistance, employee assistance program, retirement benefits, stock ownership plans, tuition assistance reimbursement, paid vacations, paid sick leave, and wellness programs.

7. **Non-monetary compensation or rewards:** These items would include things such as flexible work schedules, personal time off and recognition, parking facilities, relocation assistance, on-site health and fitness facilities, subsidized dining facilities, and continuous education facilities/support. Many of these items have value to both the employer and employee and should not be over looked or discounted when evaluating total rewards.

8. **Extra perks for the elite.** This probably fits into the category of rank has or takes its privileges. Yes, there still are things available and provided to top individuals in organizations that the rank and file do not receive and many do not even know exist. These are items such as supplemental relocation assistance, interest free loans or loans forgiven completely after a period of time, housing allowances, company cars or drivers, spouse employment support, use of company planes, supplemental life insurance, legal assistance, financial planning/tax planning assistance and yes, golden parachutes.

Knowledge is certainly power in compensation negotiations and your starting point should be to get a clear understanding of the value of the position you are considering. Recent graduates and some experienced individuals should keep their salary expectations realistic but do not underestimate your value. There are many factors that effect compensation levels and you need to consider them to bring your expectations in line with reality. You are dealing with things such as location, cost-of-living, supply and demand, industry, and type of employer, the value of the position and your specific qualifications. There is a tremendous amount of information available to assist you in evaluating the worth of career positions. A few of the internet sites are www.jobweb.com/salary www.monster.com www.payscale.com www.web.tickle.com

Analyze your compensation package as you would any important and complicated career project. The best method I have found to accomplish this is to document each direct and indirect element of compensation. If multiple offers are being considered, do a side-by-side comparison and you will be able to identify the differences. The elements will not be identical but you will be able to compare the major elements and identify differences. You will know the pros and cons of each offer.

If you are still climbing the ladder of success, consider the long-term potential of the position or career path and the organizations involved. You should also consider the level of commitment and investment the organization is willing to make in you. Since small businesses represent a significant percentage of the new opportunities, this is particularly relevant. These organizations might not be in a position to offer market competitive salaries in the form of base or cash compensation but might be very attractive long term. If you have solid confidence in the organization, its management, product and business strategies, consider negotiating for performance incentives and/or an equity ownership position. There was a time when I should have done this and this is a personal regret. Just think about the individuals who did this in the embryonic days of Microsoft, Dell, Google, or for that matter, any company you can name that is now leaders in their field. Many of them started with a few people and a good idea. The original people had the courage to take what many considered a risk, and as a result, they gained significant professional and financial rewards.

If salary negotiation is involved when making your career choice and you are evaluating multiple offers, negotiate in good faith. Your integrity and professionalism are both on display and you want that brand to remain positive. Have what you want to accomplish in mind and avoid a bidding war. Anyway, most quality organizations will not participate in extensive bidding. Identify your issues or areas of concern and communicate as specific as possible. There is a chance that your concerns might be the result of a misunderstanding or an oversight. You should also make every effort to avoid dragging the process out longer than necessary; that benefits no one. Quality organizations recognize the importance of speed and prefer to make decisions expeditiously. They like to affiliate with individuals who will get the right information, analyze the data, and move forward. Keep in mind that your compensation will ultimately be determined by the value you bring to the organization. That will be true for self-employed as well as those working for someone else. It is true that you reap what you sow in the truest sense of the words. The more you deliver, the more you will be valued. Deliver more than what is anticipated and your odds of being well compensated will increase.

Chapter Five:
You have Made Your Choice-
Hit the Ground Running

Most successful men have not achieved their distinction by having some new talent or opportunity presented to them. They have developed the opportunity that was at hand.

Bruce Marton

It is really a wonderful feeling when you have made your final choice for a position that will be satisfying, rewarding, and mutually beneficial to all parties. You are comfortable with the organization and its leadership. The content of the position is consistent with your motivations and preparation. You have confidence in the manager and feel you will enjoy working with your peers in the organization. The organizations position in the industry is established. You like your initial physical location and do not have issues with future locations as the promotions begin to occur. The compensation and benefits offer is acceptable and you have gotten a relatively good sign-on bonus. Everything is a good fit and you have decided to accept the offer and begin your new career with a progressive organization.

Accepting the offer of employment means more than just saying, "Yes, I will accept the position with the salary and benefits offered." Use this opportunity to begin building your brand in this new organization or profession. First, ask the employer to confirm the offer in writing if that has not already occurred. Most good organizations will do that as standard procedure but oversights can happen. I have seen confusion and misunderstanding of not doing so lead to bitter feelings. Make sure you have the offer in writing to avoid any potential for confusion.

Also, make sure you have reviewed and fully understand the employment contract that you will be accepting. Most people employed will have a standard employment contract but they can be very complicated for the highly rated individuals. Key positions often have complicated and very detailed contracts with a number of unique and specific elements to the individual. You will need to make a decision when you have reached the level that requires a detailed review by your legal council. You will know when that time has arrived as this is likely the time when you will have this individual involved early in the negotiation process.

Once you have your written offer and are satisfied with the employment contract, express appreciation for the offer in written form. Talk briefly about your decision process and highlight the positive things you liked about the organization that influenced your decision. Show your excitement for the new opportunity and desire to begin making positive contributions. You will welcome the positive press you will get from saying and doing things that make those already in the organization feel how confident you are about your decision. This will aid to your acceptance in the new environment.

Congratulations, it is now time to impress. You have landed the position that will jump-start your career. That is the feeling you should have if starting your professional career or making a major change. How you think is everything and you should be excited about this new beginning and the opportunities that lie ahead. Excitement drives the motivation needed to be successful. Do not be concerned if you feel a certain amount of anxiety. That is natural when significant change is occurring. After all, you will be taking on new responsibilities and will be required to interface with new people with different personalities. You have lots of new people to get to know and new processes to learn.

You deserve the position you have landed so relax and fill confident in your abilities. Obviously, others have confidence in you as indicated by their willingness to hire and compensate you to your satisfaction. The organization values you and believes you can and will do the job. You have the technical qualifications and/or experience required to perform at or above expectations. Your objective is to get off to an outstanding start. You want to show the organization is justified in the confidence it has expressed in you as an individual who will contribute.

You do want to get off to an outstanding start in your new career opportunity so begin by getting mentally prepared for what you are about to do. Review the research you completed on the organization during your selection process and make a mental note of the key relevant issues. Identify any follow up items that need clarification. If you have not received written documentation of your initial responsibilities, get clarity as soon as you can. Do not be reluctant to initiate the process if necessary. Having clarity in the early stages of your relationship will be important and can set the tone for your future success. Next, get organized. Nothing is better for insuring performance and delivering on commitments than following up your technical preparation with good organization and effective time management. Having a system that works for you is essential. Be as detailed as necessary when completing projects while in your learning phase. Acquiring the label as someone who shoots from the hip early in your career can be extremely detrimental to your long-term potential. You should also read the pulse of your leadership to determine the level of detail required to make them comfortable with what you are doing. Believe me; this does vary based on the style of leadership.

Be active and eager to learn the new activities for your position. Resist making significant changes too soon; you might avoid some major career damaging errors. Everyone will have some type of learning curve no matter how technically capable or experienced you might be. There will always be some amount of transition and you will have time to make what will be well-informed changes at the appropriate time. Speed in organizations is important but costly errors can cause significant problems. Strive to do the effective things well and with speed.

After a few days of careful observation, you should be able to identify the real fast trackers, high performers, and potential mentors in the organization. Begin networking with these individuals, as they can be significant factors in your positive transition to your new environment. Share with your new colleagues but listen more than you talk; that is how you will get information needed for your success. You already know your skills and weaknesses. What you are trying to do is learn new things that will aid you in your career development. Do not get discouraged if they do not share very much in the early days of your relationship, they will have to get comfortable with you, and that will take time.

Learn as many of the key organization policies and procedures as you can within the first week of your affiliation. Make a mental note of those unwritten rules as you become aware of them, as they exist in many organizations. You should get clarity regarding any leadership in the organization structure if it is not already understood. You will need to know the vendors, customers, processes for travel if appropriate, expense reporting, ordering supplies, procuring equipment, and any other items unique to your position.

I would recommend that you take the initiative to schedule a brief meeting with your new manager at the end of week one or early in week two. This will give you an indication of how you have preformed and the progress you have made with your initial assignments. You are sending a significant message with this approach that will benefit you later. It indicates that you intend to perform and recognize that understanding is necessary in order to make this happen. Doing this is a clear win for you and the organization as it results in needed timely communication and understanding by all parties. Keep building on your positive start and you will be well on your way to career success. Demonstrate your positive abilities early in the relationship and that will set the tone for future expectations.

Phase II: Performance and Skills Management

Chapter Six:
Performance Evaluation and Feedback

The roots of true achievement lie in the will to become the best that you can become.

Harold Taylor

Your level of performance will be one of the most important elements of your strategy for achieving career success. To accomplish this, you must keep your skills contemporary by continuously learning new methods and processes. Performance will be the equalizer that will keep your career advancing as you strive to achieve your career dreams. All businesses and organizations must generate an adequate return in order to remain viable. The results of economic evaluations are openly communicated about the return on fixed assets and total capital-in-use. We are now beginning to hear more about the return from human assets. You might not see the same level of quantifiable economic returns on the human assets in an organization but you can rest assured that the mental calculations are being made for each individual in the organization. Organizations need to be confident they are getting value from everyone in the organization in order to remain viable. The returns must justify the investments made in people, the same as required for the fixed assets.

Focus on delivering value in all that you do to insure you are an asset that is generating the desired return. There will likely be some amount of routine items in most functions but you want to focus your activities toward the high value functions and processes; those are the people identified as being special. That is the only form of job and career security in our globally competitive career environment. You must be good at what you do and simply better than your global competition. The world is getting smaller and you need to understand the real scope of your career competition. That is the only way to have career strategies that are effective. Focus on value and develop skills that are needed and transferable to changing environments. That is how you keep your services in demand.

The key question each person must ask when preparing for a performance evaluation is; why am I being compensated? That is the question you must be able to ask and answer each year throughout your career. Most individuals will have four to five key things they must consistently do to justify their continued employment. You must be able to do those things well in order to justify the investment the organization has made in you as a human asset. Before you have your formal review, rate yourself on each of those items to determine how you feel you have performed. Give yourself a grade from A to F for each major function. This will give you a feel for how you have actually performed and identify areas where you must improve. Your weakest areas are the ones that will likely hold you back. Identify those areas and set goals that will drive you to improved performance. These actions will prepare you for a performance discussion in any organization no matter how the process is administered.

All quality organizations have published policies and procedures for the performance evaluation process. It is critical that you clearly understand the rules for how these evaluations will be completed and the responsibilities of all individuals involved in the process. The employee and the manager will always have a role in the process but specific roles can vary. I have seen situations where the manager establishes some or all of the standards of performance and others where the employee essentially writes the standards with the manager or leader only modifying then approving the recommended standards. Either process can be effective; it is the understanding of the process that matters. Additionally, some evaluation processes will include the involvement of peers and possibly others in the organization as their input can be of value. Understanding the rules will be the only way to strategically manage the process and influence your performance results and ratings. You should have performance standards that result in continuous growth and learning, that is the only way to improve and advance. Routine, repetitive job responsibilities will likely keep you right where you are and will not advance your position or career.

Your performance evaluation is likely the most important process for determining your progression in an organization and your level of compensation. Your performance results are directly reflective of what you have achieved over the evaluation period. These factors influence how you are valued in the organization. I hope that you had a reasonable feel for the employee evaluation process before you joined the organization, but if you did not, do so at your first opportunity. Inquiring about this process shows that you recognize the benefits of an evaluation process and signals that you welcome the opportunity to be measured for what you do and contribute to the organization. You are also sending a message that you are an individual looking to have a career with measurable responsibilities and not someone just looking to have a job.

Prepare for your annual evaluation all year long. Keep a written or electronic copy of it in order to access it with ease. You will need to refer to it in order to make sure you are on track to achieve your agreed upon objectives. I would strongly suggest you have quarterly reviews with or without the participation of your direct report manager. It is preferable that the manager participates but some organizations do not require that frequency of formal review. At a minimum, solicit input to see if any organization priorities have changed or if some previously agreed to standards are no longer needed. Career environments can be dynamic which might require adjustments in priorities during the operating year. You need to do things that are of value and not things that are obsolete and no longer of value. If changes are indicated, negotiate adjustments and get a clear understanding about the deliverables and the time line for accomplishment. You do not want or need surprises when it is time for your formal review.

When preparing your personal standards, make sure your goals and priorities are aligned with those of the organization. Achieving personal goals that are not aligned with organizational goals will have less value. Your personal accomplishments just do not have very much value if the organization is failing to be successful. Organizations recognize this need for synergy in goals and objectives and often refer to this process as goal alignment. Everyone in the organization is working toward common overall objectives. Team standards elevate the idea of goal alignment to another level. If you have them, make sure you have an understanding of what it is that you need to do in order for the team to be successful. Goal alignment becomes even more critical when multiple individuals must contribute in order to achieve desired results.

Each employee working in an organization should have an accurate position description that is a clear reflection of his or her job responsibilities. Some organizations use generic position descriptions while others develop unique position descriptions reflective of the specific things they want each employee to accomplish. Once you have worked in an organization for a while, update your initial position description to capture any changes that have taken place. As a manager, I required that position descriptions be updated annually for my employees and expected everyone to participate in this process. I saw it as a way of continuously growing the positions and the value of the organization. The good performers understood and respected this process. Things change all the time and position descriptions should document and be reflective of the changing career environment.

Both managers and employees should be supportive of the position description updating process; it will have an impact on how positions are evaluated and rated. The rating has a direct impact on your compensation due to it being one of the documents used by compensation analyst to establish position values. The analyst also conducts a series of interviews with those who know the position content as part of the rating process. You do not want your position rating to depend on what someone hears and remembers during a verbal interview. Put it in writing and emphasize the high value elements while eliminating low value or any clerical aspects of the position, if possible. You should also highlight the things that have changed from the prior rating to insure they are included in the new evaluation. Those incremental differences can be significant and should be included for your up-dated position rating.

Performance standards are the barometer used to measure results. They are the agreed upon actions and activities that will be performed during the evaluation period. Good performance standards are specific, measurable and include a required time line for accomplishment. They should be challenging but accomplishable. Performance standards can be for individuals, a team, or a combination of both. The key to an effective system is open and honest communication by all parties. Your position description can be the starting point for your initial standards of performance. It is the basis for your core responsibilities, the essential functions for your position in the organization. Your standards of performance establish the agreed expectations for your position.

I suggest you use your standards to show your creativity and innovation by committing to do things over and above your core responsibilities. The new and high value items get the attention of your manager and other decision makers. The core responsibilities are expected from everyone, they are the minimum requirements of the position. Use this process to raise the bar and become the standard by which others are measured. Focus on those things that deliver exceptional value to the organization. Those are the things decision makers both inside and outside the organization remember, they separate you from the pack. You want the brand of being someone who is special by doing things others are not capable of doing or just do not have the motivation required to become special.

Professionals at all levels should actively participate in both internal and external trade associations. They are excellent sources for new ideas that can be implemented within your organization. I have found that most basic concepts are transferable between businesses, organizations, and industries. Things that others have done can be an excellent source for expanding your position responsibilities and making value added change. An example of this was my membership in the Industrial Research Institute Finance Directors Association. The organization held two conferences each year with participation consisting of finance leaders from at least 50 fortune 500 companies. During my term as leader of the organization, I initiated a process of having each company representative share two to three critical implementing programs at the beginning of each meeting. I quickly learned that there are very few new business problems or issues and that there can be multiple solutions for the same or very similar situations. Never resist implementing a solution to a problem just because you did not create the solution, use good ideas, and solutions no matter what the source. We found that people are willing to share solutions and are open to new ideas and concepts. Everyone gains from this approach and I am confident that continuous improvement for everyone was achieved. Sharing between organizations can be a valuable source for value added personal and organizational changes.

We live in a society of continuous change and technology is now driving change at rates greater than anything we have seen in the past. Projections are that we have not seen anything to date compared to what we are likely to experience in the future. Performance at all levels will be impacted by the desire and ability of individuals to learn and adapt to this ever-changing environment. The only way to accomplish this is to learn new processes, applications, and ways to satisfy customers. Individuals who are capable of doing this will be the ones who will be successful in their careers. Those who do not accomplish this will see their skills diminish at a greater rate than ever before. It is necessary that you keep your skills contemporary in order to be successful in any career.

There is also significant value in attending career related seminars. They are an excellent source for gaining information from industry experts in a very productive fashion. You will likely learn new methods and techniques that will be beneficial. Getting information on your own is likely to take many hours of research on your part. It is much more efficient to take advantage of what the experts already know and have researched. Also, think of the value you will get from this networking opportunity.

There is no excuse for not being able to acquire any new skills needed, as the availability of information is greater today than ever before. Information is also more current and easily accessible via the internet 24 hours per day. You can get information and tools for analyzing data in seconds for things that would have taken days, weeks or was not even possible not very long ago. Those not willing to use this efficient tool will begin to lag or not able to do many, if not all, functions required for most career fields. You cannot think about a career that has not been impacted by technology in very profound ways.

One of the processes I used in business was to have informal lunch sessions with individuals in other areas of the business from my career field who were interested in continuous learning. I found that others liked sharing the new things they had learned and welcomed new knowledge from others. Those lunch sessions proved to be excellent forums for sharing ideas and everyone gained from the experience. The more diverse the group became, the better the results. You do not want to spend all of your time with people who think, act, and have the same experiences as you. That environment does not facilitate continuous learning and you will not grow professionally. Each session would have a discussion leader to keep the process interesting and productive. Topics for discussion were submitted and communicated three days in advance of the session in order to facilitate advanced thought. No formal presentations were required but individuals did come prepared to share in the discussion. Some participants began using this group to work on skills that had been identified as improvement areas during performance evaluations. Consider this process or something similar if you feel it will be of value to you in achieving your goal of improving your skills.

Learn all you can and never stop learning. If you do stop, your skills will become obsolete and your value will diminish. Keeping your skills contemporary is the only way you can be and remain marketable. You must manage your career as a business no matter if you are an employee, contractor or self-employed. You must be able to generate a return just as any other investment or cost to an organization. It is all about productivity and shareholder value for people just as it is the case for other assets. Performance does matter; the better you perform, the greater your chances are for having a satisfying and rewarding career.

Be prepared when the time comes for your formal annual review. Prepare for this review as if you were preparing a presentation for the board of directors; it is equally important to your career success. Be able discuss what you accomplished and how the results were achieved. Talk in detail about the value which the activities delivered and how things have improved because of your efforts. This evaluation will be your formal report card. This report card should reflect what you did, how you accomplished the results, the quality of the effort and if the results were delivered within the agreed timing. The formal appraisal system will possibly classify this as situation, behavior, and result in order to identify accomplishments. Use this opportunity to suggest and encourage frequent feedback on your performance. This will make future reviews easier and more efficient. You should also use this discussion time to talk about your career aspirations. Talk about the things you like about your current position but also your thoughts regarding your career goals. The leadership in your organization needs to know what your future desires are and you should take the initiative to communicate your thoughts. Having career goals that are not communicated will not get you what you want from your career.

Candor is essential for all involved in the process in order for an evaluation process to be successful. Some managers have a difficult time being completely honest with employees and that is unfortunate. You do not gain anything when the evaluation is not done with candor, desired development will not occur. If you are not being told about your areas of improvement, you cannot improve. If your manager is not being honest, take it upon yourself to identify the areas you feel need improvement; you will certainly know. I hope that you will not encounter a manager who is not being fair during your evaluation process but it could happen. If it does, have the courage to stand up for your performance and do so with facts. That is why you should keep good, accurate records of your accomplishments and their impact on the organization. Having facts can be your best asset when resolving differences of opinion. Never agree to unsatisfactory performance results when the evaluation has not been fair and truthful. Work to get a satisfactory resolution and never agree just to complete the process. When items become a part of your official record, they essentially become fact.

You should also be mindful that informal reviews occur all the time. Always be able to talk about the major priority projects in your portfolio. When participating in general discussion, be able to discuss the high value projects that require you to do new and innovative things. Whenever possible, do things that involve and positively affect customers because you always want them to say good things about you specifically. Being customer sensitive is always positive as organizations recognize that without customers, they have nothing. Take your blinders of when thinking about the concept of customers. Everyone in any career field or service area will have customers; they do not have to be in a direct buy/sell relationship to qualify as a customer. Delighting your customers will increase your value to the organization while defining or supporting your personal brand.

Make sure you get what you need from your performance discussion in order to be confident that you are on track to achieve your career objectives. There are key ingredients for an effective performance evaluation system. Focus on the following and you improve your odds of getting what you need from the process.

1. The review and discussion must be with candor and complete honesty by all parties.
2. You need measurable, good quality performance standards that are challenging but fair.
3. The evaluations must be completed timely and you must have adequate time to complete the assigned projects.
4. You need to have open and on-going communication to avoid surprises at the time of the formal review. Strive to create the type of relationship where you can ask how you are doing at any point during the performance cycle.
5. You must make sure your evaluation has been fair and is an honest reflection of what you have done and accomplished.
6. Performance objectives must be aligned vertically and horizontally in order to be effective. That is how you achieve high impact results.

The format for performance evaluations vary by organization but most have many of the same major elements. Organizations will want to document performance with some level of detail and have a summary of the results that is easy to understand and access. What follows are examples of typical formats used for the performance evaluation process.

Employee Evaluation
(Example Only)

Name: Department: Employee Number:

Position: Position Rating: Evaluation Period:

Dimension: Assessment

Situation:

Behavior:

Result:

Signature:

Employee: Leader: Approval:

This evaluation will likely list four to five specific behavioral examples. Those examples should be the higher value items that affected the results of the organization positively or negatively. The intent is to describe what you did and how the results were accomplished.

Employee Assessment Summary
(Example Only)

Strengths: Written communication
                            Analytical skills
                            Leadership
                            Attention to detail
                            Technical translation

Development areas: Delegation
                            Persuasive ability
                            Presentation skills

✓ Action plan: More frequent communication with manager to review on-going attention to needed areas. There will be external training that focuses on professional selling skills and effective presentation skills.

Performance rating: 2 (Distinguished)

Promotability: 2 (Ready in 1 to 2 years)

Potential: 2 (Minimum of two levels above current position)

360 Degree Feedback

Individual departments are no longer isolated and able to operate independently. Effective organization structures operate without boundaries that often require individuals to interface with and be effective in a number of environments. Independent line and staff organizations are outdated. Current technology allows individuals to work effectively from just about anywhere and with anyone. Performance evaluation systems have recognized this and a number of organizations have implemented a 360-degree feedback system to support the employee evaluation process. This is a supplement to the traditional evaluation process done by the immediate manager. Input is received before the formal employee discussion with the manager in order to have the value of more and broader perspectives. A number of progressive organizations have adopted this process as a more effective tool for improving performance. Advances in technology have been able to facilitate this process while maintaining the required confidentially.

The employee, in conjunction with the manager, solicits performance input from the employee's peers, subordinates, and other mangers of which he or she interfaces. These individuals are involved in the day today actions and the immediate results of projects. They should have valuable insight regarding what and how performance results were accomplished. They should have an opinion regarding major strengths and development areas. You need to know what these individuals feel about your performance and the results you achieved. The manager will have the responsibility to assess the validity of the data provided, as there can be conflicts or differences in opinion about job performance. At a minimum, the impressions will be known and any issues about performance can be resolved.

You might have some level of discomfort with this process just as I did. My initial thoughts about it were negative. I did not want to be evaluated by my peers, subordinates or some leader I might not be on the best of terms with. I guess I was concerned that they would have something negative to say and I would not appreciate negative comments. After thinking about it with a more open mind, I was more comfortable with the concept and supported it with enthusiasm. I found the results of the process to be positive and of value. I received useful information that I was able to act on and improve my performance. If you had issues with someone or some process, it is best that they are identified and resolved.

If something surfaces during the process that is not legitimate, corrections can be made. You have the opportunity to address false or incorrect impressions in a productive way. Perceptions are reality; they are the same. It is much more productive to know the opinions others have of you and the quality of what you do than not. Embrace this process if formalized in your organization. If it has not been formalized, get input from others on an informal basis. You will likely gain even more respect and admiration from those you care enough to ask for input. People like to feel that their input is valued especially when not required. Use the input wisely to improve your performance, value and ultimately your personal brand. Do not be surprised if you create new friends and allies because of this process.

Chapter Seven:
Career Coaching

Life consists not in holding good cards but in playing those you hold well.

Josh Billings

Contemporary thinking regarding performance improvement frequently looks to professional coaches as a method for achieving continuous improvement. If you do not use a coach, use your evaluation process as a way of accomplishing essentially the same thing. You and your boss should always have a common objective of making you a better performer each day. Both of you have significant investments in the process and want positive results. Your boss should have experience in a number of areas that should be beneficial to your growth and development. Seek out the coaching and guidance needed to achieve ever-improving results. If your boss does not manage the process to facilitate natural coaching, take the lead to make it happen. He or she will be able to do it because it is somewhat natural once the process begins to flow. Help facilitate the information flow by doing the following:

1. Clearly communicate your personal desire to improve in all that you do.
2. Let him or her know that you are willing to put forth extra effort in order to get better.
3. Communicate your respect for other perspectives that might be different from yours, particularly from those with more and broader experience or specific expertise.
4. Volunteer to take any available continuing education that will aid your professional growth and development.
5. Ask for guidance on any available industry trade associations in order to stay current with industry or professional trends.

6. Show initiative by personally researching and discussing ideas for self-improvement that you have discovered.
7. Follow up during the year with any new ideas you have regarding ways to improve. This sends the message that you do think about improvement at times other than the formal performance evaluation.

Effective coaching is a tool for getting improvement from existing employees. Employee turnover and poor performance are significant drains on productivity that is extremely costly. That is the reason why there are major incentives to make employment relationships effective once they have begun.

I do not often use sports analogies but in the case of personal coaching, I will make an exception. I currently reside in the Columbus, Ohio area and this is Buckeye country. I have never lived in an area with more loyal football fans than The Ohio State University. The recruited players generally respect the winning tradition at the university and willingly accept coaching. They also recognize the need for continuous improvement. The current head football coach is Jim Tressel and he always talks about getting better each week. Once he established that culture, the entire team embraced that powerful message. Nearly 100 percent of the time during interviews, the players will articulate their desire to *"get better each week."* They articulate that message whether they win or loose. They talk about improving when they win by a large margin or a small margin, it does not matter. The entire team believes in the continuous improvement process and supports the coaching philosophy. Your career is certainly more important than athletic competition but you can use coaching as a means for improving. It will aid you in leveraging your preparation for career advantage. Strive to get better each day and use all the tools needed to make that happen.

Most individuals will encounter performance issue at some point during their career. It does not matter how competent or educated you are in your profession. The odds of your total career being smooth sailing with no bumps in the road are not very good. At some point, you are likely to have some type of difference of opinion regarding concepts or techniques for achieving objectives. In some instances, the conflicts might be as simple as a personality difference or it could be something more significant. I had my share of issues to deal with and most likely, you will as well. Do not be discouraged or depressed if it happens. You are not the first and certainly will not be the last to have to deal with something unpleasant. In some ways, it is surprising that it does not happen more often given business complexities and all the diverse personalities that must function together.

When you are faced with situations related to performance issues or business results, the worse thing you can do is ignore them or become non-responsive. Ignoring the situation and hoping it will self-correct or simply go away just will not work. That will only make things worse and the delaying will only add to the difficulty of the situation. Performance issues require action to change reality or perceptions; there are no other options. I have personally found and observed that the best practice is to be forthright, recognize the issues, address them, and move on. Procrastination and ignoring the problems only allows them to grow and become more difficult to resolve; never make a bad situation worse. Instead, begin a viable strategy to turn the situation around in a positive way. I know I have said on many occasions that businesses or organizations should stop spinning information and just tell the truth. When difficult issues are not resolved, they will only grow and you cannot make progress.

Think seriously, about what you plan to say before you put your feelings about performance issues in writing. Think carefully about the things that need a written record of any kind. Learn to do this early in your career and let it become a skill that will serve you well. This will keep you out of trouble in more ways than you will ever imagine. Just think about the number of times you have said or done something that you later wished you had not. Think about the number of things you have written that you have secretly said I wish I could take that back. Once you put it in writing, it is now documentation that cannot be disputed.

Communication is the key to resolution when all parties have the same objects and want successful outcomes. That is the only way everyone wins. Complete candor is the only policy that is effective long term. Individuals and organizations that do not believe in this practice will have difficulty being and remaining competitive. Truth and honesty are the only platforms to stand on; there are no exceptions.

Chapter Eight:
Communication Skills

The impossible is possible when people align with you. When you do things with people, not against them, the amazing resources of the higher self within are mobilized.

Gita Bellin

Superior communication skills are essential for all outstanding performers in most any profession. In fact, I can say with certainty that I have never observed anyone known as a top performer who did not have good communication skills. Written communication skills seem to receive adequate attention in most academic curriculums; they only need to be practiced and fine-tuned in the professional environment. I do not feel oral presentation skills get the attention they deserve given the importance in the work environment. I have frequently seen presentation skills listed as an improvement area during human resource reviews for a significant number of individuals. I initially thought the identification of presentation skills as an improvement was just a convenient or easy improvement area when the manager could not identify something more job specific. That might have been the case in some instances, but in most cases, the assessments were correct. Objective thinking and experience has taught me that most of those evaluations and assessments were right on target. Most individuals are average to below average when it comes to presenting information and really connecting with their audiences. It takes training and practice to make an impact when given the opportunity to take center stage and present information to an audience. Only a select few individuals really master the art of becoming an outstanding presenter or orator.

If your desire is to be a valued performer or someone at the very top of your profession, it is essential that you develop superior presentation skills. Everyone can overcome their deficiencies in this area through training and practice. Some individuals might have natural skills but they are the exception. Most outstanding presenters of information have been trained on the specific skills and techniques while practicing their craft frequently. Once you have knowledge of the techniques, the more you practice, the better you get. You can see measurable changes as confidence builds because of actively practicing this craft. Be honest with yourself about your capabilities as a presenter because you know and recognize your own capabilities without being told. You will know if you are proficient or have deficiencies in your presentation skills. It will be to your advantage to improve if you need to and most of us will have some room for improvement. Those who recognize this and take action will begin separating themselves from the pack. I needed and wanted to improve and actively worked on developing the required skills.

Do not believe you can develop outstanding presentation skills without some amount of specific training. You can improve and make some amount of progress by self-study and practice but your rate of improvement will be slower and you are likely to develop some bad habits that are difficult to change when you do know better. Unless you are that rare individual with the natural and instinctive ability to make outstanding presentations, give yourself the value of formal training in order to develop the good techniques that will support your improvement efforts. Your skills will only get better as you practice while you gain more knowledge and experience in your profession. Having the knowledge without being able to present it effectively is a waste. Following are a few ideas from my formal training, research, and observations that I have found useful for making good presentations. This will hopefully get you started and encourage you to get more training in the area of presentation skills if needed. It is always better to take action because of a self-assessment rather than waiting for someone else to recommend a training need.

1. **Know your subject matter:** This allows you to speak with confidence due to your depth of knowledge and understanding. You will be able to deliver your message with confidence without memorizing every word or depending on detailed notes. You have command of the subject and are in control of your thoughts. Omitting a few words or statements will not get you off track and you have less concern regarding flow of the information. Your thought process and flow can be supported with a few bullet points.

2. **Powerful opening:** Have a powerful opening that sets the stage for the remainder of what you are going to say. Let it express your

passion about what you plan to say by showing your commitment to the effort or activity. Smile and use good body language that supports the engagement of the audience. When you do this, your odds of getting everyone's attention improves significantly.

3. **Preparation:** Nothing can take the place of being well prepared to deliver your message. This allows you to have thoughts about any potential questions that might arise because of what you have communicated. You will be able to respond quickly and with confidence. You will be in control of the message and the direction you are trying to influence.

4. **Information flow:** Prepare an outline and decide on a logical flow for your material. Try telling stories and keep a fluid flow for your information with specific powerful emphasis where needed. Know when and where you want to say or do something that will be remembered by everyone.

5. **The audience:** Know your audience well and know whom you need and want to influence. Get the audience involved and they will be additional support for the message you are conveying. Listen, connect with your audience, and never loose their attention. Move around as you connect with the audience but do not allow your movement to be distracting. Share and relate personal experiences that support what you are saying. Make and share eye contact, it makes everyone feel important. You give the impression that you are talking to them on a personal basis and not just a presenting to a group.

6. **Keep it simple:** Stay on point during your presentation and keep the message as simple as possible. In most instances, you are likely to know more about the subject than anyone in your audience but there is rarely a need to let them know. Share the specific details if requested but do not let that side track you from what you are trying to accomplish. Make an effort to minimize the use of numbers, as they are likely to confuse some in the audience. Convert them to pictures or trends if possible.

7. **Avoid distractions:** Avoid the distraction of using notes or too many slides or bullet points. You want the audience looking at and connecting with you and not your visual aids. You want to show them your passion and commitment because of your body language and expressions.

8. **Practice:** Practice your presentation using a live audience if possible. Do it with a trial audience that will be critical of what you are saying and have no reservations about telling you the

truth. You are doing this in order to be the best you can in your live situation so honesty is certainly to your advantage. This will allow you to do any fine-tuning before the official presentation.

9. **Relaxation:** Arrive early to the site where you will be presenting and make sure everything is set up for your delivery. Make sure all equipment is functioning as desired, the lighting is appropriate and that the room is laid out to accommodate the attendees and your needs for delivering the information. After assuring the room set up conforms to your needs, begin the relaxation techniques that work for you. I personally use deep breathing exercises followed by a bit of personal meditation. You must be relaxed in order to have any chance of delivering the message you want. If you are nervous and stressed, you will not have a smooth flow and you will not be connected with the audience. If you are nervous, the audience is likely to read this as a lack of confidence in what you are saying. Your audience will look for errors or will ask more questions about what you said.

10. **Powerful closing:** Leave your audience with something they will remember that is special. Ask for any support you need if appropriate and realize when you have gotten closure. Thank them for their attention and support.

I have developed these techniques because of formal training, practice and the need to present information to various type audiences for years. The more you are required to present, the better you will get at making formal and informal presentations. You simply get more confident because of doing. Everyone can improve no matter what your current skill level. Some individuals will need more specific training and practice in order to improve but the results will be noticeable as your techniques and skill level evolves. These techniques will also aid you when required to talk spontaneously without the benefit of formal preparation and practice. Many of the learned skills will become natural and that is what you ultimate want.

Phase III: Career Strategies

Chapter Nine:
Career Path Planning

A good plan violently executed right now is far better than a perfect plan executed next week.

General George Patton

Career path planning is the process of establishing a clearly defined plan to achieve your career goals. The process should be implemented with the same level of discipline you would use for an important business plan. Most career paths will have some logical number of prerequisite positions leading to the top position in the profession. This process is similar to what you would anticipate having for an educational curriculum for a field of study. The process requires that you successfully complete assignments at each level before moving to the next logical position in the career path. You build on your experiences and leverage each to facilitate the career progression. Performing at each level will give you confidence as you progress toward your ultimate goal. When opportunities arise, take advantage of them, and believe that you can and will perform at each level. Use the psychology of performance to your advantage. Believe in yourself and that you will perform at each assignment during your career. Motivated individuals with adequate skills can and do rise to the challenge when given opportunities to advance. I have found that this is true even when the positions were somewhat of a stretch given the candidates background and level of experience.

Is it possible to make progress without performing functions at each predefined level? You absolutely can! It is not an easy thing to accomplish, and you might not have the instant respect of your peers, but you certainly can be successful. Good performers gain the respect of everyone in the organization by performing. I found that I rose to the level of the challenge during my career, and you can as well. Have confidence in your abilities, and you will be just fine. If you need to work harder and smarter, do it. If you need to acquire new skills in order to perform at your desired level, get those skills and build your knowledge base. Following are the elements of career path planning I found useful for evaluating, monitoring, and achieving career path objectives:

- ✓ Performance accomplishments
- ✓ Continuous learning, skill building and training
- ✓ Networking
- ✓ Mentoring
- ✓ Correcting identified development areas
- ✓ Self assessment of performance and progress
- ✓ Time line for promotions and key positions in the career path
- ✓ Career plan adjustments as required

Monitoring these elements will allow you to keep an accurate record of the progress you are making toward achieving your career objectives. Develop a matrix or tracking system that you feel comfortable using that is simple and easy to administer. Put your review dates in your calendar and have the discipline to complete the necessary reviews. You might think a 30 or 35-year career is a long time but you will be surprised how quickly the time during your career will pass. You do not want to wake up someday feeling that it is too late to follow your dreams and accomplish what you had planned to do years earlier. Planning will aid you tremendously in monitoring your progress to allow adequate time to take action.

Most career fields will have a logical career path of positions that successful individuals have held leading to the ultimate position in the profession. That is the person who sits in the big chair with the corner office with lots of windows. Always believe the playing field is level and that everyone has a legitimate opportunity to be the leader of the organization or business. It is a fact that if you do not believe you can, you want. Nothing has ever been achieved that was not believed possible. Moreover, the surest way to failure is to stop believing and trying. Never let anyone kill your dreams of getting to the top of your profession. Stay flexible and adjust your plans as needed because things can and will change. Let us look at a couple of traditional career paths for the areas of finance and sales & marketing.

Career Path Progression
(Example Only)

Finance	Sales & Marketing
CFO	VP Corporate Marketing
VP/Controller/Treasury/Tax	VP Marketing Division
VP Division Finance	National Sales Manager
Director Audit	Marketing/Product Manager
Accounting Director	Regional Sales Manager
Operating Area Controller	Sales Manager
Finance Manager	Sales Supervisor
Division Finance Analyst	Advanced Sales Representative
Financial Analyst	Sales Associate

Be mindful that career paths will vary by organization, industry, business size, and structure. Additionally, these are examples only as there are numerous other career options in these professions. In finance, you can have a career in areas such as investment banking, insurance, stock analyst or broker, financial planning, auditing services, tax preparation or many other areas. A similar list can be developed for most any career field for the multiple choices available. Keep an open mind and do the required investigation to find your area of interest and your motivation.

Organizations are becoming flatter with levels and positions being eliminated or significantly changed. Traditional organization structures are being changed because of restructuring, operations streamlining and technological innovation. These factors will continue to have an impact on the number and type of positions available. Organizational development has now become a major function in many businesses with productivity being the emphasis. You must stay current with changes that are occurring within your career field and plan accordingly. As organizations become flatter, the people who will be in demand are those who are flexible, innovative, embrace change and will do new and progressive things. You can fine more information and resources to aid you in career path planning on the internet at www.ewin.com .

Recognize Your Value

In order to maximize your career potential, it is essential that you recognize your true value and worth to all potential organizations and clients. You should keep a daily or at a minimum, weekly diary of your contacts, experiences and value added accomplishments. First, you will be surprised at the things you do that are of value and secondly, you will have a wonderful source of information to keeping your resume fresh and up-to-date. If you do not keep this type of documentation, it will be difficult for you to recall all the wonderful things you did and accomplished during the course of your career. We simply get too busy doing to remember all the details. If you delegate the score keeping to others, they might be inclined to remember the things you did not do rather than focusing on your accomplishments. This just might be the result of having very different motives for the scorecard. If you do work for someone else, you need the data to support your recall during performance reviews.

For some reason, most of us have learned or been trained to think less of ourselves than we actually are in reality. We often think of it as boasting or bragging when talking about ourselves when we posses skills that are special and not common to others. If you are guilty of this negative thinking, you must change and learn to think and act more positive about your accomplishments, strengths, and abilities. You must learn to act and present a positive, self-confident image in order to become a special, high performing individual. That approach sends the message that you are worthy and ready for any challenge that comes your way. Others will begin thinking and talking about you in positive terms relative to your professional acumen. This will be of significant value to you personally as well as the organization for which you are affiliated.

We often devalue ourselves because we only see things through our eyes, not through the eyes of others who might have done and accomplished much less. This devaluing seems natural so we simply must learn differently. The differences in abilities occur for numerous reasons: education, experience, longevity, exposure, aptitude, attitude, or just simply greater interest in a particular subject or profession. To put this in perspective, just think about the number of times you have been in a personal or business situation and silently said to yourself, I thought everyone knew that or I thought everyone did it that way or I thought everyone could do that. How many times have you been in a situation where you discovered that there were things you had experienced or done years before others? You mostly likely looked at many of these individuals as peers but realized that you had more knowledge and experience than others you know and respect. The more you know about and understand your career competition, the better prepared you are to achieve and accept success.

One of my career experiences with this was my participation in a global trade association, The Industrial Research Institute Finance Directors. The participants were from around the world and employed by major companies in very diverse industries. I quickly learned that there are very few, if any, new business or finance problems or issues. I also learned that there could often be several solutions to what on the surface appears to be the same problem. Additionally, I learned to feel good about what I had personally done and accomplished over the years. This experience reinforced my value and worth to my current and possibly other organizations. From an internal perspective, I felt that our list of things to do was very long and wondered if we would ever get everything completed. From an external perspective, I learned that my list of accomplishments was significant and compared favorably with other leaders in industry. I certainly had a better appreciation for my personal talents and abilities. Feel good about what you have done but do not depend on what you did in the past to sustain you during your career. If you do, someone else will set the standard and you will be struggling to catch up.

One way of monitoring your personal value is to establish standards of performance versus peers. By doing this, you will be able to quantitatively judge your accomplishments, level of performance, contributions, and comparative value to peers. Do not be overly concerned with the level of accuracy because that is not critical. You are dealing with an order of magnitude and the worse case scenario is that you will have more comparative information than before. You will either get more confidence and appreciation for your personal abilities or recognize that you might be falling behind versus peers in your profession. Honesty about what you have done and are capable of doing is essential for this process to be of value. Once you see where you are versus peers, do not be afraid to raise the bar. Someone will do that and it might as well be you. Set the standard in your career field and be the one by which others are measured. Always strive to leverage your knowledge and experiences in order to enhance your career opportunities. If you are falling behind, take action to get better.

For a business or employer, you are an investment. The more you return, the more you will be valued. That is your only form of position and career security. Invest in your education and skill building; they will assist you in your need to add value. Your beginning education and initial skills are sunk costs. The marketplace will not pay you if that is all you have to offer. Your continuing ability to be compensated will be driven by the value you contribute.

There is no such thing as job or career security in today's business and professional world. The odds of joining or starting a company and have it last an entire career are not very good. Individuals who work within a single organization for 30 or 35 years then retire are and will be in the future, very rare. Most individuals joining the workforce today can look forward to having three to five different careers with some being in very different industries and/or organizations. The rate of change will be greater in the future with new industries emerging and some current industries becoming obsolete and going away. That is life in a rapidly changing world driven by information, technology, and continuous innovation. There are some survival skills that you can utilize which will keep you valued and your services in demand.

1. **Be valuable:** Some individuals are obvious keys to an organizations success. They are the people others, including key decision makers, go to for solutions. They are capable of doing things others cannot or will not do. They have unique skills that are not possessed by others. They have established unique relationships with customers or suppliers and have countless allies. Without them, functions will be performed, but not without a loss in productivity. Strive to have a niche that makes you a valued resource to your organization.

2. **Be embraced:** You should strive to have broad support from others you work with outside your organization. Community involvements, as well as industry, are both important factors in how you are perceived.

3. **Be an innovator:** Unless you are working in a totally machine paced environment, there will be times when your normal, routine job responsibilities are not required. This presents an opportunity for you to distinguish yourself by being innovative and showing your creativity. Use these times to raise the bar by doing something new. Focus on those high value projects that have taken the back burner while the routine business activities had to be completed.

4. **Communicate:** People often have good ideas but just keep them to themselves. Communicate what you have developed in

effective ways in order to get your ideas implemented. If you are not sharing your quality ideas, concepts and solutions with others in the organization, the things you know will not translate into value.

5. **Embrace change:** Having a comfort zone can make us feel warm and comfortable in most any environment. Remaining in your comfort zone can be detrimental and it is an obstacle to any change environment. Nothing will stay constant in business or organizations and those who embrace change with enthusiasm improve their odds of being successful. Change is career enhancing by providing the opportunity for you to be involved in new and innovative ventures.

By doing these things, you have not only increased your value to your current organization and career, you have also made yourself more marketable. You have gained new skills and techniques that are transferable by participating in the continuous learning and development process. If one door should close for some reason, another will open if you have kept your skills contemporary.

Be Receptive to New Opportunities

It is essential that you are receptive to new career opportunities no matter what the source. You might see an advertisement in the newspaper or on the internet. If you are networking effectively, chances are, an opportunity might present itself when least expected. Networking is also a process to get exposure to positions before they are advertised. These sources could be friends, family, classmates, peers, business associates, clients, neighbors, members of boards you might serve on or competitors; the list is endless. Learn to utilize your sources effectively.

When an opportunity presents itself, immediately turn off those negative tapes and turn on the positive messages. That was a hard lesson for me to learn. I had an opportunity to join a dot com organization in the embryonic stage of its business cycle and all those negative tapes turned on immediately. I thought I would be taking a big chance and I had family responsibilities to consider. I thought about the technology not working or being received well in the market place. What would the competition do about a small start up? Would existing large, established companies dominate this small start-up company? What would I do if the venture failed?

Rather than thinking in all those negative terms, I should have been positive and followed my true feelings. I felt that this was outstanding technology with great potential. The process was superior to anything I had seen and we had looked at all the logical competition in this market as part of an evaluation process. The leadership was outstanding and had a good record of accomplishment in the industry. I could see myself working with this organization and having fun. Yes, there would have been challenges but that is what I liked and wanted at that stage in life, a new challenge. I got pleasure from delivering solutions to business problems and that is exactly what I would have been doing. Sure, I would have to learn some new things but that would have been fun and exciting as well. It would have required a move to California at some point but I liked that part of the country and it would have been a refreshing change. I had confidence that I could and would have done well with this venture.

I did not make the change because I made a poor decision and listened to those negative tapes. I determined that it was too risky for all the wrong reasons. That is the power of negative tapes. They totally dominated logic and reason and that happens much too often. My quality analysis essentially meant nothing. I feel impelled to tell you what ultimately happened with that venture because it is exciting.

There were about 20 people involved in the company when I first had contact with the organization. My first meeting with them was in a conference room about the size of the average family room. They had about five beta sites for the software product they were marketing and were looking for more. The salaries of the people were low by most standards, but they all had equity positions with incentives for additional stock options each year. The company went public about nine months later and I am tempted to say that the rest is history, but there is more. The product is now global and they have at least 5,000 employees with a significant revenue stream for product sales, royalties, maintenance fees, and services. The product offering has been expanded with no signs of slowing down. The product now takes full advantage of the internet and that opens up even more opportunities. Most, if not all of the original people have moved on for various reasons but left as millionaires a few times over. The stock price has seen continuous appreciation that has resulted in several stock splits. This type scenario will make you wonder about the road not traveled.

My guidance is that you avoid being risk-adverse and resistant to change. Change is going to happen so you might as well plan to manage it while following your dreams and good instincts. Do not listen to those negative tapes that tell you that you cannot do certain things and that you are not worthy. Remember that you are as prepared and as worthy of success as anyone. You have prepared yourself, learned continuously and are ready for the challenge. If you do not try, you have given up the opportunity to succeed. Sometimes the biggest risk is the risk not taken.

Chapter Ten:
Career Development

A step in the wrong direction is better than staying on the spot all your life. Once you're moving forward you can correct your course as you go. Your automatic guidance system cannot guide you when you're standing still.

Maxwell Maltz

The higher you move up in an organization, the brooder you will be required to think and act. You will be required to manage diverse functions and areas as your responsibilities increase. This requires specific knowledge and training or at a minimum, some amount of exposure to a number of functional areas. Management skills are relatively easy to transfer but you know the technical aspects of a position or you do not. Can an individual manage an area or function without being technically competent in the function? Absolutely, it has happened in the past and will likely happen in the future. Will there be challenges? In many instances, there will be. I have seen successful leaders and failures with either approach. It depends on the individual and their attitude as well as willingness and ability to learn. Good management skills combined with a strong staff to support the manager, increases the potential for success.

Some organizations have adopted a process to give individuals with long-term potential broader experience by providing cross discipline training and exposure in the form of specific assignments. If you have this opportunity, seize the moment, because it is a signal that you are a serious candidate for more responsibility. Individuals fortunate enough to have this unique opportunity are expected to do the job they have been assigned. They must not look at it simply as a training or exposure assignment. Giving the perception that you are just there to learn the ropes will get no respect from those whom you will be working with and the process will be a failure. You cannot send the signal that you are special nor have unique privileges. It takes teamwork to get things done and individuals who look at themselves as special are not team players. Anyway, there are usually no guarantees of a time line and it should be understood that the individual must be successful in the assignment or the relationship could be over. I have actually seen terminations when individuals perceived to be high potential but did not perform to the desired level early in the professional relationship.

I witnessed one of these programs in action early in my career. There were five highly educated finance individuals hired in what was labeled a "fast track" program. They had outstanding technical education credentials but limited or no practical experience of significance. The initial program using this concept was a disaster. Most individuals in the program really thought they were special and were likely given signals from the organization that reinforced that thinking. Most of those individuals never really engaged themselves in the organization. Several took the money, training, exposure and moved on within a year. We learned from that experience and made changes in the program for high potential development and exposure.

We found that the keys to a successful accelerated development program were communication, selection, program definition, and follow-up. The program must be well communicated to everyone in the organization and there must be a good understanding of expectations by the individual, manager, and peers. Selection of the participants is extremely important because the person must have the right attitude and personality to make this approach effective. The individuals also must enjoy the work environment that they have been assigned. If they do not, others will know because this is something that you cannot fake. I have seen sales and marketing professionals assigned to technical areas or manufacturing operations with the assignments turning out to be a disaster simply because their personalities just did not fit. Other similar assignments were made with outstanding results. The approach can work well when done properly.

When I had responsibility for this type program, I required that the assignment and specific work activities were clearly defined and communicated. The individual knew the job they would be performing, and the expected results. A learning curve for anticipated results was established for each task to make sure the program stayed on track. We had scheduled follow-up sessions and reviewed results with leaders in the organization. Some participants were also given broader assignments to evaluate the effectiveness of the knowledge building process.

Anyone wanting to advance their career should take advantage of broad training and development programs when available. They have proven developmental benefits that are career enhancing. You will get outstanding experience while acquiring prerequisites for future opportunities. As a caution regarding cross-functional moves, make sure you understand what is in the move for you and the organization. You are managing your career and the assignments you accept must be compatible with your dreams and goals. You do not want to make a move that is not consistent and supportive of your long-term desires. Do not be lead to a position or career choice that does not fit with your career objectives. Do your homework and understand the technical and managerial backgrounds of the individuals holding the position to which you aspire. You do not necessarily have to mirror those career paths because things can and do change but there should be some logic and consistency.

You must also be aware of what the current trends, practices, and emerging technologies are in your profession. When rapid change occurs, which is the case in most professions today, your skills can quickly become obsolete. If you fail to stay current, you could find yourself reporting to someone who at one time reported to you because organizations promote individuals who perform and can deliver the most value.

An excellent way of keeping your skills contemporary is participating in business and professional trade associations. Make every effort to identify progressive organizations that are innovative and focus on leading edge innovation. Actively participate when involved with these organizations because you are always building your brand and expanding your network of influence. Remember that all contacts and chance meetings can be future opportunities for personal and professional growth. Keeping your skills contemporary will be an asset to your current position and will enhance your marketability. It is the only way you can keep moving toward achieving your career goals. Be mindful that everyone you meet could be a learning experience. Learn from your manager, peers and yes subordinates.

After keeping your skills contemporary, do not forget to keep your resume fresh. Keep it current by updating it periodically to reflect your ever-developing skills and accomplishments. This should be done just as you would plan for a performance review, it could be equally important. Always be able to talk about what you can and have done during the course of your career. Make special note of the high value items and those requiring innovation or resulted in major change. You need to do this because you never know when you might have to land another position by either choice or chance. After all, good performers can be out of a job at any time due to no fault of their own. You need to keep your options open, particularly in our rapid changing environment. Put this in perspective by thinking about the number of restructuring, acquisitions, outsourcing and other changes we hear about that essentially mean the business will now operate with fewer people. You are for all practical purposes a free agent with skills that are marketable. There are no guarantees of permanent career employment in any area so you must keep yourself marketable.

It would not be appropriate to leave the discussion on career path planning and development without challenging you to consider non-traditional careers as an option. I know I certainly would have had I known more about them. Do not limit your career path choices to those obvious fields that everyone seems to select. Those positions are listed in the newspaper or posted on the internet and there is likely to be a lot of competition. You can possibly do well in those positions but you really must be exceptional due to the amount of competition for the available positions. Staying challenged long term in routine positions, if there is any such thing anymore, will be difficult and require lots of innovation on your part. Those are also the positions that are prime candidates for automation or process changes.

Do yourself a favor by searching out those unique career opportunities that others often either do not know about or just do not find attractive for some reason. You might discover an opportunity that will really get you excited. Your self-assessment should give you some insight to aid you in your selection process. You should also think about the numerous products or services you use or have been exposed to for career ideas. Analyze the processes required to get those products or services from manufacturer or source to the consumer. You might discover a career opportunity of which you might not have been aware. If you do not understand the many functions in the process, take the initiative to investigate the business, career field, or organization. Start with the internet then make the research as personal as required to get the information you need. Set up meetings with key individuals in the business or organization and interview them about career opportunities in the industry or profession. Most people enjoy talking about what they do or know and are willing to share their knowledge and experiences. You could meet someone during the process that could turn out to be an asset to you and your career.

I have now met a number of individuals who are doing things in non-traditional areas. Many of them have proven to be very interesting and they seem to be satisfied by both the professional and financial rewards from their career choices. Many have found that their skills are being utilized effectively and they enjoy the variety of activities. It is possible for some of those niches and less visible careers to be just what fits your needs and desires. Who knows, you might end up with an ownership position that you never anticipated. Be open to unique career opportunities; they could prove to be rewarding and personally satisfying.

Chapter Eleven:
Relationship Building

To be successful you have to be selfish, or else you never achieve. And once you get to your highest level, then you have to be unselfish. Stay reachable. Stay in touch. Don't isolate.

Michael Jordan

The saying that no man is an island is true relative to your career just as it is in life. During your career, you will be required to interface with people of different genders, races, ethnicities, cultures and sub cultures. Society is becoming more diverse every day, requiring that we all become more understanding and sensitive to other ways of thinking and acting. It is simply a professional need and requirement in order to be successful at what you are doing or plan to do. With the internet and ease of international travel, contact with individuals of different backgrounds has become very common. Given these facts, we all need to find effective ways to operate in this relatively new and exciting environment.

My initial exposure to the cultural differences as a professional was primarily the Western European cultural differences versus American. Moreover, it was primarily associated with manufacturing, sales and marketing. Things are now much different as the world has gotten smaller and business is now global in the true since of the word. We must relate to and interface with others around the world performing numerous functions and activities. Anything that does not require face-to-face contact can be done virtually anywhere and by anyone. In fact, a number of services which many of us would believe are being done domestically have been moved off shore and are now being done seamlessly. This puts the need for and skills required to build relationships into a very different perspective; it is a fundamental requirement for a growing list of professions. Be sensitive to this and do what is needed to be effective during your career.

It is very possible that you will develop life long friendships with some individuals because of your career affiliations. However, that is not your primary objective of building business relationships. If it happens, that is terrific. If it does not, you still must be able to be effective in your career even when working with others whom you have very little in common and no personal relationship. During my career, I worked effectively with some individuals whom I really had little in common with personally. It was nothing personal; we just were not interested in the same things outside of the work environment. I had trouble with this for a number of years and I am sure it affected my job performance. Looking back on the situation, I would have made some changes in my approach. I now know much more about the importance of relationships. Most of all, I have learned that people are who they are and it is a major waste of time trying to change others. The real objective is to understand others and utilize the correct strategy to achieve what you desire from the relationship. Embrace this idea and you will certainly be more successful in your career relationships.

Since you cannot change, what others say and do, work to change how you react in those situations that push your buttons. I finally learned that the attitude you have about the individual and situation you are dealing with will affect how effective you will be in dealing with others. Your first order of business is to stay calm and rational. This will allow you to stay focused on your true objectives of the relationship. Avoid the immediate temptation to strike back when faced with career conflict. Some people count to ten in order to delay their response when someone has done or said something that has upset them. I have begun asking if this will matter in one, five or ten years. It helps me put things in perspective and allows for more controlled reactions. Once you put situations into the proper perspective, you are more prepared to deal with what ever comes your way. Think about the situation you are confronted with in relation to some difficult time in your life. You will fine that most situations during your career will not rise to a level worthy of damaging an otherwise good relationship. Think twice before you speak, think twice before you act and you will go a long way toward managing your relationships.

You will encounter many different people during your career. The differences in level of achievement will come from motivation, preparation, opportunity, and their ability to build relationships. Once you have found your niche and become good at what you do, you will need good relationships in order to maximize your opportunities. You will get things done with and thru people; it is just that simple. How you interact and react to the many different personalities you encounter will be a major defining factor in your career success. This will be true no matter what level you are in the organization. I have found that it is best to stay focused on your real objectives and adjust your reactions to others in order to remain effective. Learn more about relationships and dealing with people by reading, *"Dealing With People You Can't Stand"* by Dr. Rick Brinkman and Rick Kirschner. Do not be confused by the title, the book has outstanding information needed in order to work effectively with people. You might be successful without having good relationships but it will certainly be a lot tougher.

Networking

Networking is continuous and not a project that will be completed with nothing more to be done. As long as you desire to build and grow your career, you must continue to grow and expand your network of valuable contacts. Your contacts should be individuals who are growing and making an effort to strive for greater success just as you are doing. This might mean that some contacts in your network have to be eliminated or at a minimum become less important over time. This by no means or implies that you will become too important for people who have been good friends and supporters over the years. It only means that you both may have changed and have different priorities. People do grow at different rates and have priorities that might not be compatible. As you grow professionally, you want adders in your life supporting you and you them. When your network is filled with individuals with mutual interest, you will not have time for negative contributors or diversions from your objectives and goals.

Be aware that networking opportunities happen all the time and not just during formal business or social settings. You never know when a chance encounter might lead to a wonderful career enhancing opportunity. Those encounters can initially happen at an athletic event, on an airplane, in the grocery store, at a department store, at a restaurant, at the office supply store, at your place of worship and yes, over the internet. It can happen anywhere you go and have contact with others; the potential for networking is unlimited. As a result, always think about the impression you make on others and the conduct you display at all times. First impressions are made about people within the first three to five seconds of meeting. That is right, people have formulated some type of opinion about you just that quickly so work on making a good first impression by the way you initially interact with others.

Once you have made your initial impression, learn to interact with others in positive ways. Start with making a good physical impression and show that you are approachable by your facial expression and body language. Practice smiling and greeting others in the way you want to be greeted and addressed. Make conversation with individuals you do not know, they might turn out to be someone you want as part of your network. You always have the option of changing the relationship but do be open to expanding your network of contacts. Be selective and make your decision regarding future need for interaction by learning to read others and their interests. I do not mean to suggest you stereotype, as that can be a major negative for networking as the world is becoming more diverse. Treat everyone you encounter with dignity and respect, you might learn some interesting and positive things about different cultures. I personally feel my life is much richer because of meeting and getting to know others from different cultures.

After making your initial networking contact, learn to have the type of conversations that are mutually beneficial. You are not in the relationships only for what you can get from others. You must give in order to receive so make sure the process is balanced. Networking is much more than being introduced to someone at a meeting or social event and calling the next day to ask for a position or recommendation for a job in their organization. Networking relationships requires an investment in time and effort. They create win/win relationships between deserving partners. True networking relationships should be nurtured and allowed to grow over time. They can also expand as others are brought into the process because of mutual interests and goals.

Staying in contact with those in your network is easier now than ever. In this age of electronic communication, you are able to stay in touch with very little effort. However, do be mindful that the quality of the contact is important so make sure you are sharing worthwhile information. Show that you are working to make the relationship fruitful and mutually beneficial. Do not limit the communication to just electronic messages. Determine the type of communication you want to have based on your personal judgment. Personal contact is certainly important at times as it presents unique opportunities. It can be a wonderful idea to invite someone in your network to participate in social functions, continuing education sessions, or personal growth initiatives. You would be showing that you care by offering to include others important to you in meaningful career related events.

I have found that sending hand written notes are an excellent way of staying in touch with those important to any network. I have sent some for very special occasions while others have been sent without specific cause or occasion. Those notes have much more impact when they are being sent when you are not asking for anything. You are sending it for them, so be genuine with what you communicate. Just think about how you personally felt the last time you received a hand written note from someone special in your life. The memory will last for a very long time. Begin doing it and your network of contacts will likely reciprocate by doing the same with you and others. You might start a positive trend with those you have allowed to have a front row seat in your life. Spontaneous phone calls can also aid in the process but the impact is not as long lasting. I have known individuals who would put reminders in their calendar with alerts to remind them to make those contacts. Do it if it works for you, you will certainly enjoy the benefits from the effort.

When someone in your network does something special for you, be sure to acknowledge the action and express appreciation. Your network functionality and results will be diminished if you fail at effective nurturing. An example of a situation such as this recently occurred for me personally. I became aware of two outstanding positions that seemed perfect for individuals I knew well. I made them aware of the positions and sent all pertinent contact information. One individual did let me know that she received the information and had begun the process of contacting the organization for follow-up. She expressed appreciation for the information provided and thanked me for thinking of her for the position. The other individual has yet to mention anything about the communication. The appropriate actions would have been to acknowledge receipt of the information and express appreciation for the thought. A follow-up with some type of status reporting would have shown her thoughtfulness for my action. If not interested, a polite thank you would have been sufficient. All she had to say was that the position was not for her but please keep her in mind if you see something you feel would be a fit in the future. This would have required minimal effort and the career networking would have remained functional. You never know what the next identified opportunity might bring.

Networking is a vehicle that can be effectively used to your advantage as you grow your career and personal contacts. Use your partnerships wisely and never take them for granted. There must be a balance, which means you must give in order to receive. Be visible and stay well connected within and outside of your chosen career field. You never know when a good opportunity might come or from what the source will be. Be approachable and know that those chance encounters just might be the opportunity of a lifetime.

Mentoring

There is significant value in the mentoring process for both the employer and the protégé. Statistics show that the retention rate for new hires increases for employees who participate in mentoring programs. Individuals with good mentors perform to higher levels than those required to succeed without the benefit of a mentoring relationship. Organizations look at people as assets and they see real value in improved performance from the process. Successful mentoring processes improve the odds for organizations getting the desired value and return from their investments in people. Organizations want individuals who are hired to succeed and deliver the anticipated value.

An effective mentoring program is needed for employees of all skill levels. This is true for new entrants into the work force as well as those with years of experience in the same or a different industry, business, or professional discipline. Every organization will have written rules, many of which will be documented in formal policies and procedures. There will also be unwritten rules that are critical for success in most any profession. A good mentor, who well understands those rules, can be an extremely valuable resource. They can provide guidance on critical issues affecting the organization and your career success.

During my career, I have actively participated in a number of mentoring programs with all having the objective of creating higher performing individuals and organizations. Some organizations have general mentoring programs with others being structured along functional lines. Either system can be effective for achieving improvement in the performance and success of the participants.

I have also been involved in a more advanced form of mentoring that was identified as an executive development program. This program would assign an individual, who was believed to be high potential, to an executive level individual. This senior mentor would spend a significant amount of quality time with the individual while also making sure the protégé was getting challenging work assignments. They would often be given assignments in multiple disciplines as part of their overall development program. This type of program can really accelerate your career development. If you have an opportunity to participate in this type program, seize the opportunity.

A high percentage of organizations now have formal mentoring programs but if your organization does not, informal programs can be effective as well. Do participate if possible in some type of mentoring program. If no formal program exists, do not hesitate to approach a desired mentor that you feel confident about regarding being your mentor. People do like to help others and often find the process personally rewarding.

I suggest you have a mentor inside your current organization and one out-side your primary organization. Have back-ups in mind for both as things can and will change over time. You never know when your mentor might leave the organization, become out of favor or when the relationship simply might not work out over time. Your outside mentor can provide a valuable external perspective on professional and developmental ideas. Just think of the significant changes that have occurred in a number of industries and you will see the value of diversifying your support base. Anyway, you are likely to have multiple careers and chances are; they will be in different businesses, organizations, or industries.

Following are the characteristics I feel you should look for in a good mentor.

1. The individual must have a sincere desire to be a mentor.
2. The individual should take pride in seeing others achieve career success.
3. The individual should be well respected and connected in the organization or profession.
4. He or she should really understand the value of mentoring and support the program with enthusiasm while being committed to making the program successful.
5. The mentor should know the written and un-written rules in the organization or profession and be willing to share his or her non-confidential knowledge.
6. The mentor should have a history of personal success during his or her career and in the profession.
7. The mentor should be a broad thinker and a visionary in the profession.
8. The mentor must be a good communicator.

For any program to be successful there must be something in it for all individuals required to make it work. People simply must get in order to give with enthusiasm in most any situation. We live in a society that expects a pay off and mentoring is no exception. Following are a few of the many things a protégé will get from a mentoring program:

1. A potential portal to career success
2. Needed career information driven by years of success and skill development
3. Support when needed and often least expected

4. A strong ally and positive role model
5. Potential career opportunities for available positions before they are known and/or communicated to the public
6. Accelerated career development

Following are the things the protégé must do in order to have the mentoring relationship deliver maximum value.

1. Perform to the very best of your ability and deliver solid results
2. Be dependable and never disappoint your mentor
3. Be appreciative of the efforts of your mentor and let him or her know that you sincerely appreciate their support and involvement in your career
4. Be visible and communicate frequently while being respectful of your mentors time and career responsibilities
5. Be supportive of your mentor and the things he or she are endeavoring to accomplish
6. Never exploit your relationship by demanding or asking for unrealistic things
7. Be selective when openly asking for favors or preferential treatment. Always maintain integrity in the relationship and keep it professional.

Following are the things the mentor will get from the relationship.

1. A dependable ally and someone you can depend on for support
2. A good performer and someone you have personally assisted in developing
3. Personal satisfaction of seeing performance improvement
4. The personal satisfaction of giving to others
5. Respect from peers and subordinates as a developer of people
6. The personal knowledge that you have done the right thing

The mentoring process is a professional relationship between two colleagues. The experience of a mentors support can be powerfully positive and enabling for the protégé. Having a successful program will require that roles are clear and that candor is the rule for communication. Regular reviews and discussions are strongly encouraged in order to support the program. You will get significant value from your participation in the mentoring process; use it to your advantage as one of your strategic career management tools.

Chapter Twelve:
Career Changes

The world hates change, yet it is the only thing that has brought progress.

Charles Kettering

Outstanding careers do not just happen; individuals who strategically manage their careers create them. These individuals look for opportunities and have the courage to act when opportunity arrives. They learn continuously and take calculated risks that facilitate their "luck." They listen to those quiet voices that give them positive direction throughout their career. They believe in the psychology of performance and have a positive, can do attitude–they simply believe they are worth of accomplishing their dreams.

It might be necessary for you to overcome some negative tapes in order to aggressively manage your career for maximum success. We enter life's journey with a clean slate and an open mind then proceed to place restrictions on ourselves in much of what we do. When we are born, we have only two fears, the fear of falling, and the fear of loud noises. Studies have shown that the conditioning begins in early childhood and continues until the individual decides to make a personal change. That is likely why the term comfort zone has received so much attention. A number of programs have been developed to help make us more receptive rather than resistant to change. We often refer to the process as breaking paradigms in order to facilitate change. I believe we have been programmed to look at change and risk only in negative terms. That is unfortunate and not enabling for successful career management outcomes.

Let us start with how the term risk is defined: 1. A source of danger, a possibility of incurring loss or misfortune. 2. A venture undertaken without regard to possible loss or injury. 3. The probability or likelihood of an adverse effect or event. 4. Expose to a chance of loss or damage. These are the definitions of risk we have become accustom to seeing. Is there any wonder why we feel that risk should be avoided? This is likely why we find such comfort in staying put and not embracing change. This very well could be why we have such anxiety about change, particularly those related to a job or career. Could this programming be why we do not follow our dreams of starting a business and believing it will be successful? I believe this is the result of looking at risk only in these negative terms.

There is another side of risk that is very positive. There is a good chance that you will get what you want. There is a good probability that you have prepared yourself for success and that it will happen. You just might have done the needed analysis, planning and documented the strategies and tactics to be extremely successful in your professional endeavors. Removing the psychology of performance is a clear step in the right direction. If you do not believe you can, you want.

It would be much more satisfying and rewarding to think in terms that reflect achievement. Let us review the definition of achievement: 1. The action of accomplishing something. 2. Successful attainment of goals. 3. Ability to demonstrate accomplishment of some outcome for which learning experiences were designed. 4. To accomplish a task or objective. I feel it would be more advantageous to focus on the things that could go right when considering something new and different such as a career change. Find ways to erase those fears and objections that we develop over the years and you will improve your chances of realizing more dreams. Career changes can be rewarding and personally satisfying when approached properly.

Reflecting on what I felt was a risk early in my career really was not very risky at all. It only seemed like a risk due to the negative tapes from my programming. I was a financial analyst in a manufacturing environment. I had financial responsibility for several production departments and the process and technical organizations. The organization had a philosophy of continuous improvement and we were constantly looking for ways to improve productivity. Most projects required involvement from several disciplines in order to deliver results.

I was presented with a proposal from a manufacturing engineer that would dramatically change one of the manufacturing processes. The production manager supported and felt good about the idea. The only problem was financing, and if I could find a way to handle the cost of the investment. It would not conform to our normal financial scrutiny due to it being very experimental. We did not know the actual returns and cash flows from the proposed change. I did know and understand the potential benefits of the proposed process changes. I had confidence in my team member's abilities and they had a record of successful accomplishments. I knew that the worse case possible was that the process would improve to a level that was more efficient than what currently existed. It no longer seemed like much of a risk.

We invested the required capital in the project without the normal approvals. The process worked with a payback in about four months, which was an exceptional return. The new process was adopted for the entire organization and there are now several facilities using that basic concept. It was not a risk but an opportunity to make real productive change. Maybe there is something to the saying that in order to get the fruit, you must go out on the limb.

Taking calculated risk is what I feel is the right approach. Do your homework, have a strategy supported by a plan, do not procrastinate, focus, implement with speed and you improve your odds for success. These were many of the things those surveyed talked about as what facilitated their success. Many of the business owners had worked for companies of various sizes and had gone on to start their own businesses. They were able to learn from established businesses then transfer those skills to their new careers. That seemed to be an excellent approach to learn from practical experience while getting prepared to follow your true dreams. The more diverse your experiences, the better chance you will have for future success. I caution you to be sensitive and not abuse your opportunity to gain experience. Place a priority on performing the functions you have committed to doing for the organization you have joined. Always act with the highest degree of honesty and integrity in all that you do and never take unfair advantage of your career situation. Your first priority must be to perform the functions for which you are currently being compensated.

It is very easy to secure employment with a company or organization and get very comfortable. We know the people, processes, and the job and feel good about our professional progress. I am mindful of the man who started rowing a canoe miles above Niagara Falls. It was a beautiful day and he was enjoying the scenery. He decided to take a nap only to be awakened by the roar of the falls. That is a very good analogy of how fast time will pass during your career. You need to stay constantly aware of the progress you are making on your career plan. You do not want time to pass, leaving you with an unfinished career agenda. Dreams are not followed and you might end up with regrets about what you had planned to do but did not accomplish.

During my research for this book, a number of relatively successful individuals had some regrets about not evaluating and possibly pursuing other career opportunities. They regretted not expanding their horizons more, learning diverse things, contributing more and deriving more satisfaction. Several talked about the feeling of having, to some degree, an unfinished agenda. They talked about wondering what their career and life would have been like had they made a few different decisions about their careers.

I received survey input from one individual who was an outstanding performer whom I personally respect highly for his professional capabilities. He was employed with one firm for 25 years in a number of capacities. He had held a number of positions in Human Resources, Labor Relations and Benefits area. He had progressed well and made significant contributions to the organization. His career had been successful by most standards but there was something missing. I also have the impression that his contributions were not respected and appreciated as much as they should have been. He decided to pursue a change in his career after 25 years. He is now very satisfied with the change he has made. He felt that he should have made the change several years earlier. I think there is a lesson in his experience about analyzing and deciding when a career change might be appropriate. He is now motivated and more excited about his career than he had been for sometime. He likes the new challenges and the new location has turned out to be a pleasant change.

I am not suggesting that you should never be satisfied and constantly look for a change in position or career. I am saying that there are times when it is appropriate for you to consider making a change in companies, organizations or your career. It makes logical since to test the market when you are serious about a change. Be mindful that this is another reason you should learn continuously, keep your skills contemporary, and your resume fresh. Your contemporary skills are more transferable than most would believe so have confidence when you decide to make a career change. We often think of making a change in employment or our career as taking a risk. It is not the degree of risk we anticipate. Life after a change can prove to be very satisfying both professionally and financially. Do not hesitate to make a change when the time is right for you to do something different. Procrastination can be detrimental to achieving your dreams. Test the market when you feel the need to do so and you just might find a rewarding career opportunity.

When making a change, you will need to learn some new terminology, new people, and possibly concepts but the learning curve will be much less severe than you would anticipate. Just think about it without your blinders and the fear normally associate with risk and all will be fine. Put it in the perspective of the anxiety and the learning curve associated with your first venture into the workforce and the situation will look much different. It makes sense that you as an experienced individual would be able to adjust and function well in a new environment. You now have the tools to make an immediate impact and you owe it to yourself to do exactly that. With experience, you gain a wealth of wisdom that is much more valuable than most individuals realize.

In business and careers, it is important to recognize when it is time to move on. This should not be taken personal because everyone's time will eventually come. The need for change does not necessarily reflect anything bad or negative about the individual, it is just time for something new and different. The new challenges can be ways of recharging your career and making your days more exciting. Just think about how exciting it can be to learn new processes, get to know new and different people, a new organization and location, and possibly in very different part of the world. All of this can be very rewarding and personally satisfying.

My experience tells me that you will know when it is time for a change and the signals will be clear. You might initially resist them due to the natural instinct to remain in your comfort zone. Some of the early warning signs that it might be time for a change are:

1. **Fun:** You do not seem to be having the fun you had when you joined the organization. The time you looked forward to the next interesting challenge has been long forgotten.
2. **No new learning**: You feel you have mastered all the things the position has to offer. You have innovated as much as you can, given the boundaries that exist for you within your current organization.
3. **Your boss**: You have lost respect for the person you report to and no longer feel comfortable communication with that individual. Your beliefs and philosophies are in conflict with his or hers.
4. **Wrong area:** We often enter careers or accept positions in organizations for the wrong reason initially. That is probably why you see numerous individuals working in fields that are outside of their areas of training and education. Recognize when this has happened and take action to find the career that fits your motivation.
5. **Dread Monday morning:** You hate the fact that the workweek is starting again. You have nothing to look forward to other than the weekend and cannot wait for Friday!

Think about these symptoms when evaluating your career situation. Do not let the small bumps in the road influence you to make a change too soon but if these things persist for an extended period, a change might be appropriate. When you do decide to leave, utilize a strategy to do so, just as you did when joining the organization. It is equally important and in many ways, more important. You now have more experience and will be looking for something better. When you do decide to leave, consider the following:

1. **Have a specific plan:** If you plan to secure another job, that will require a resume, skills evaluation, networking, interviewing, recommendations and all the things you did to acquire your current position. If you plan to start your own business, you have even more preparation work to do and that will be discussed later in more detail.

2. **Negotiate your separation package:** There are policies on this but everything within reason is negotiable. Moreover, if you do not have a new position, which is the best option, you will have to support yourself financially during your transition.

3. **Never burn bridges:** Do not feel you should settle all scores just because you are leaving. That solves nothing and does more to hurt you than the organization you are leaving. I cannot think of any advantages of leaving on a negative note. Instead, think about the positive things you have experienced during this phase of your career and the interesting people you have met. Think about the numerous things you have learned and will take with you into the future. Let these thoughts guide what you say when leaving.

4. **Leave with dignity:** It is important that you leave with dignity and self-respect. Moreover, as much on your terms as possible as the problems that are now influencing you to leave have grown over time. This should be possible if you read the signs as you should. Do not get emotional; stay under control and do not say or do something you might later regret. Remember to always think twice before you speak, think twice before you act.

How you make changes is so important that it deserves more discussion. You should develop a philosophy that you will never burn bridges no matter if you stay with an organization or decide to leave for other opportunities. Inexperienced, emotional and vindictive individuals can often do major damage to their potential career opportunities by the actions they take when making or considering a career change. The damage is sometimes done verbally, delivered through others or with written words. The opportunity is seized to let those in authority know all that is wrong and the problems they should fix before others leave the organization for greener pastures. You make the management team aware of the many reasons the competition is performing so much better and why the market share has been on such a downward trend. You let them know that the Research and Development people are worthless and have not developed a good product offering in years. The finance people have not been creative and really destroyed the financial reporting capabilities with the latest system conversion.

Yes, you really let them have it! However, what did you really accomplish with all the steam you let off? You have now become the topic of conversation in the cafeteria, at a dinner meeting, in the halls, rest rooms, the company picnic, staff meetings, during trade associations, officers meetings, the human resources department and with peers in other organizations. All this will occur within about a week or two of you letting them have it. Now you have really been successful and have gotten your name and approach published to all the internal and many potential external employers or future business associates. Do not forget how wide the reach is for your networking and remember that it works for positive and negative events. You never know when you might need someone to say something positive and supportive about your personal or professional acumen.

Rather than burn all those bridges by talking about all that is wrong with the organization you are now leaving, think about all the good times. Think about where you were on the professional learning curve when you joined the organization versus where you are now. Think about how strong your resume will be now that you have experienced so much and had the opportunity to train and manage others. Your value has increased significantly because of your many experiences and these experiences will aid you in gaining employment or starting the business you have been considering. Additionally, your previous employer and related contacts could be a source of revenue for your possible business opportunity.

I think you have the picture but let me be very clear on this issue as it is just that important. Say nothing in conversation or in your written letter of resignation that you might later regret. Write the letter, rewrite it once or more and proof read it carefully. Read it for clarity, content and the ultimate message that it sends. After you are satisfied completely, have a trusted friend that you respect highly regarding professionalism, vision, judgment, and wisdom read it to get their impression of what you have said. Be comfortable with the way you are communicating that you will be leaving the organization. You gain nothing from putting the organization down by blowing off steam. You have an easy decision to make in how you choose to say you are leaving. Leave on a positive tone and you have left the door open just in case you might want to return in the future. After all, there had been many things you liked about the organization when you made the decision to join it initially.

Finally, keep everything you are dealing with in perspective. You will experience many more things in life that are more significant and important than a job or career change. The earlier in your career you realize this, the better, as it will serve you well and aid in your decision processes. No matter how bad you believe you have it, there are many more in the world doing much worse. Be confident when making career changes and believe you are worthy of following your dreams. When you decide to make a change, move on with confidence and never look back.

Chapter Thirteen:
Career Challenges and Opportunities

Finish each day and be done with it. You have done what you could; some blunders and absurdities have crept in; forget them as soon as you can. Tomorrow is a new day; you shall begin it serenely and with too high a spirit to be encumbered with your old nonsense.

Ralph Waldo Emerson

During your career, there will be periods when you feel that you are growing professionally and contributing immensely each day. You will feel that there are not enough hours in the day and you cannot wait to get back to your work environment to do and learn more. You have a significant learning curve but things are exciting and each achievement is personally rewarding. New opportunities to contribute surface every day and you see no end to the potential for your position and career growth. The business or organization has tremendous demand for the services or products and growth is projected to be positive for several years. You feel good about your decision to join the organization and all is well.

Fast forward about five years and things have changed. You have mastered the learning curve for your initial assignment and the two promotions you had received. You have done your best to come up with new things to do but nothing seems to be worth the effort. Additionally, the growth in products or services has slowed significantly to a level only equal to growth in the overall economy. No new facilities or products have been developed and new support projects have been placed on hold indefinitely. Fewer people are being hired so the requirement for training others, which you liked, is no longer needed. A few years can make a significant difference in terms of career satisfaction. Situations can and will change.

There is a chance this might happen during your career and you need a strategy to first identify the signs of potential frustration or burnout and then be able to take corrective action. During good economic times, you might have more to do than time available. During softer business or project conditions, downsizing, restructurings and the resulting fear of job loss, the physical stress can lead to possible burnout. Some of the signs of burnout you should look for are:

1. **Anger at management**: You are likely to ask yourself; how did they let this situation happen? How did they allow the demand for our products and services to decline as much as it has? Why did they reduce research and development to the level that resulted in no new products or services? You essentially have concerns regarding the motives and competencies of the organization's leadership.

2. **Chronic fatigue**: You no longer feel strong and confident. You feel constant exhaustion and tired. You feel physically sick and have to fight the urge to avoid the business environment in any way possible.

3. **Cynicism:** You are more negative than you have ever been and it has become obvious to others. You are irritable and hostile to individuals you have had positive relationships with in the past.

4. **Self-confidence:** You are beginning to question your personal worth and contributions. You are beginning to feel helplessness.

5. **Hostility:** You explode easily because of insignificant things. Your relationship with peers and other team members is beginning to decline.

6. **Health:** Your health is being impacted such as frequent headaches, weight gain or loss, loss of sleep, depression, and elevated blood pressure. You just do not feel well and relaxed.

If you experience any or all of these symptoms of burnout, immediately take steps to address them, as they will not self-correct. Preventing or eliminating job burn out requires both individual and organizational change. This is often misunderstood resulting in the focus being on the individual and not the issues associated with the organization. As a result, the primary focus has been on teaching stress management techniques. This approach recognizes that individuals cannot control what happens to them but they can control how they behave and respond. Burnout can be contagious and if left unchecked, it could possibly spread through an entire organization. I have witnessed this and the turnaround can be difficult. You will see individuals talking about how awful their situation has become at every opportunity. You will hear comments about the unrealistic job demands, poor management decisions, and failure of management commitments. It will seem that everything is wrong and nothing is right.

In order to defend against being part of the problem, you must be personally engaged in the organization with a focus on solutions in order to turn the situation around. Do not play the all is wrong game and contribute to the problem. Focus on the things you can positively affect and encourage others you interface with to do the same. Welcome any available training to help you cope with the difficult times. Focus on the activities that give you personal satisfaction. Reassess your values and make sure you have the balance you need to be effective. Learn to pace yourself and avoid personal frustration. Moreover, take care of your personal health because without it, nothing else matters.

Some organizations have it all wrong and never admit or recognize that the organization must change in order to have a complete solution for burnout problems. Several years ago, I worked for a firm that was going through a restructuring because of a hostile take over attempt. The stated objective was to make changes that would provide more value to the shareholders than what would be delivered by the acquiring company. The first question that logically comes to mind is if the organization was being managed well by competent management, why had not it achieved better results in the past? Why did it require the threat of a take over attempt to facilitate value added change? The leadership team decided to find a way to retain the "good" performers by creating an attractive stock incentive program. I guess it was a form of buying loyalty and commitment. As part of the celebration for this new class of employee ownership, there was a boat trip down a river with a festive atmosphere. That new group of employees was known to the ordinary people as, *"the boat people."* They had been chosen to receive significant rewards if they stayed with the organization during the transition. The leadership team just did not get the fact that an organization needs complete engagement of all people during good and especially difficult times.

Rather than doing what was required to get everyone engaged and focused, the organization had created a defined class structure. There were the boat people, the chosen frozen; I love you for now, and those who would be terminated. Most in the organization had it all figured out and knew where they stood in the new structure. There was also the problem of politics in how individuals got into the various classes of employee and that was an issue. No matter what the official records say in human resources, the people in the organization know who the real contributors are and have strong feelings about them.

This is an example of how the actions of leadership can cause cynicism to spread like wild fire then become the norm. Individuals who had always been positive turned negative. The work force was reduced but none of the work went away. Some reports that had not been used for years were still required. The burnout got worse and the attitude of not caring existed throughout the organization. Things did not really change until a significant portion of the management team was replaced. It took a different team with a very different philosophy of how the organization should be managed in order to improve moral and correct the burnout problem. Engagement resulting in self worth was the answer. We began to see an organization that was high energy, effective and delivering solutions.

If faced with burnout or any of the symptoms, you will have decisions to make. Do the things you can do but also observe the organization to see what changes are being made to facilitate the needed corrective solutions. Look to see if the current management team is really changing or doing the same things while hoping that they will get different results. Look at the processes to see if they are different. Evaluate the strategic and operations plans to see if implementing tactics support the objectives. If you are not seeing real change and you continue to suffer the terrible signs of burnout, it might be time to market your skills to another organization that is more compatible with your goals and expectations. Your life and career are much too important to spend unnecessary time suffering the ills of career burnout.

The one constant you can always count on in life and your career is change. No matter how well you analyzed the organization, its leadership, markets, and competition; it all could change overnight. That can also be the case for the person you directly report to in most any organization. You start your new position and everything is the way you had imagined. You immediately develop an even better relationship with the manager than you had anticipated. The work is exciting and you have been able to bring in new ideas that resulted in an immediate impact on the results of the organization. You have good people on your staff but they have some development areas that you can affect. They are willing to accept new ideas and you like the challenge and satisfaction from the rewards of helping others. Life is good!

Three months later, the plant manager you had such a positive relationship with announces in the staff meeting that he had been promoted and would be relocating in one week. He indicates that he does not know who his replacement would be but did have a good idea. Most of the staff had a good idea as well and we did not like the answer. We were pleased that the current manager was being recognized for his work and getting promoted but did not like the traits of the likely replacement. Following are some of the new manager traits that were just the opposite of the departing manager:

1. **Low value:** He believed in doing things that kept people busy but had little value and impact on results. Few would ever know or care if many of the things he wanted done were completed.
2. **Panic:** He would panic about things that were not significant or critical at all. A simple phone call or message from someone of authority could result in numerous projects. Opportunities for value added activities were missed while doing low value projects.
3. **Do it my way**: He stifled creativity by wanting to do things the way he was accustomed to seeing or having them done. Innovation was not the focus.
4. **Style**: His desire was to manage professionals as if they were machine passed production operators. Results seemed not to matter just that the project or program had been worked on for hours or days.
5. **Must be right:** He rarely allowed himself to be wrong or accepting of a new approach or way of doing business. He often delayed value added implementation due to over analyzing in attempts to prove himself right.

This happened to me and it just might happen to you at some point during your career. My guidance to you is do not panic and act in haste. In many instances that could be the worst thing you could do. After all, the only thing that has really changed is your direct manager. What you will have to do is develop strategies to deal with the new manager in different ways than you had with the previous manager. Most situations are manageable and this is no different. Obviously few have gotten this message because the boss remains the number one reason people leave positions.

The first thing you must do is get support from trusted peers. Chances are that if you are facing these issues, many of the same things are probably affecting others. Do not use this as an opportunity to bash the boss and the organization by talking about all that is wrong, use it constructively to develop and/or share strategies to deal with the new management style. It is your career that you are managing and you do want things to work out positively. You should also use your mentoring and networking contacts as a source of information, strategy, and wisdom. In my personal situation, I had this due to my relationship with the new manager's boss. As a result, I was able to be effective in the relationship while providing council to others in their approach to this new management style. Use your imagination and you will come up with solutions. Functional people, who might be located in regional or central offices, can be a source of information and influence.

I would also caution that you should not always believe what others tell you about a manager and his or her style. What others say is their personal opinion and you just might experience something very different. You could have a different experience for a number of reasons and just might relate very well to the managers style and ways of doing things. My experience in this regard was with the comments made to me by others about an individual who became chief executive officer of the organization of which I was affiliated. Several people had told me that he was difficult to deal with, demanding, unforgiving and impossible to satisfy. My actual experience indicated that he was kinder and more understanding than advertised, intelligent, worked hard, paid attention to detail, had a clear vision, expected results, earned respect, supported his organizations completely, and never asked more than he was personally willing to give. We had many of the same traits and we had a good professional relationship over the years. He was also fun to be with socially.

You should give any management situation a chance to work. You might be surprised how an anticipated bad situation could turn out over time when objectives are clear to everyone. Things often are not what they seem and that is especially true in career situations. Even in diverse situations, we are more alike than different and certainly can learn from each other. The other thing you can count on is, after all storms, there is calm. I have learned that all things will pass so be patient.

The road to success in your career will not be straight. There will be curves called failure and curves called confusion. If you are faced with either of these, look at the situation only a bump in the road to success. Do not dwell on unpleasant situations and let them distract you from achieving your goals. Learn from both the negative and positive experiences then move on as you follow your dreams. Do not let the difficult times be your defining moment, be defined by how you respond. Respond in positive ways that address meaningful issues no matter how difficult they may seem on the surface. Avoiding or pretending that problems do not exist will only allow them to get worse.

No one likes to talk about the potentially most difficult bump in the career road, which is termination. That can be the most significant thing you might have to face given the ever-changing business and professional world in which we now live. I have personally known and interviewed a number of individuals who have dealt with employment termination. Many have moved on and had very successful careers in the same or a different field of endeavor. The lesson I learned from my research and surveys was that seemingly bad things sometimes happen to good people. I also found that these temporary bumps in the road could happen when the reason has nothing at all to do with the individual involved. Do not take it personal, the situation might not have anything to do with what you have done or failed to do.

To put this in perspective, think about the number of businesses that have been acquired, experienced a leveraged buy-out, gone bankrupt, or experienced the many economic cycles or the emergence of competition that was on no ones radar screen. Businesses and organizations have been known to reduce the size of their work force for these and other reasons in attempts to deliver more value to shareholders. There can also be a business culture and/or management change that results in terminations. When leadership change occurs, the new leadership often brings in their team of support people. Managers like to work with individuals they are comfortable with and know.

If faced with this situation, keep in mind that an employer does not define you. If you can look up, you can get up. Do not dwell on the past and what went wrong. Immediately get moving and look forward to the future. When a change occurs, an opportunity happens at the same time. It is a time for reflection and plan implementation. Get busy working toward those wonderful things you will do in the future. If you need professional help with your efforts to transition and move forward, get it as it can be of value as you set the course for the next phase of your career journey.

Chapter Fourteen:
The Dream of Business Ownership

Everything is always impossible before it works. That's what entrepreneurs are all about–doing what people have told them is impossible.

R. Hunt Greene

Failing to follow the dream of business ownership was the most frequent regret sited by the professionals in the survey I conducted for this book. Many felt they had an entrepreneurial spirit and had dreamed of running their own business but had failed to take action. They talked about their desire to have the control and make a real difference but never got around to implementing their ideas. Some had even developed plans and strategies but just did not execute. A number of reasons were given for the reluctance to pursue their business ideas such as fear of failure, lack of feeling secure, believing the idea had too much risk, not being sure of the projected profitability, family responsibilities etc. When you look at the failure statistics for start-up businesses, they can be cause for concern relative to the ability to be successful. Data shows that half of small businesses fail during their first year of operation and an even greater percentage fail within the first five years of operation. If business ownership is your true dream, you do not have to be one of the negative statistics. You certainly can be successful by employing effective strategies while pursuing your dream of business ownership.

Most individuals will likely begin by working for some type of organization before branching out on their own. There are some exceptions but to begin your career as a business owner will happen in rare instances and in certain fields of endeavor. That is the case for new start-up businesses. Those fortunate enough to enter a family or some other on-going enterprise represents a much different scenario. If you do begin by having employment in some organization, it is possible that you can use that experience as a springboard for your business venture. Naturally, your first priority is to perform the functions you are being compensated for by that organization. That is your ethical professional responsibility. However, you can use that experience to learn and develop many of the skills that will be essential for you to be successful in your future business venture.

The idea of business ownership is no longer a large factory employing thousands of people. It is no longer a multi location manufacturing or retail operation, which once employed a high percentage of the population. With the transition to the information age, which is being driven by the internet and a variety of devices being used to access information, the game has totally changed. Many of the new businesses often do not require any brick and mortar. In fact, fixed assets in some respects can be a significant liability with things changing so rapidly. You will find that many of the new businesses are one or two person operations that are often home based. There are advantages to starting the small home based operations and allowing it to grow and expand as the markets being served dictates. The ultimate ability of any business to grow internally is based on the rate of return on equity. Growth above that will require either equity or debt financing.

Running your own show can be extremely rewarding but it will certainly require significant commitment and lots of hard work on your part. Before you make the move to business ownership or deciding to freelance as an independent, ask yourself the following questions in preparation for what you are planning to do:

1. Do you have a marketable product or service in mind that will be in demand for a reasonable period? You will need customers who will buy your product or service when you put out your open for business sign.
2. Have you gotten key professional credentials and industry accepted approvals needed to validate your product or services to potential clients or customers? Have you gotten all needed federal, state, and local licenses for your planned business venture?
3. Do you have a credible, detailed business plan that is reasonably accurate? Have you done sensitivities for your business plan for both optimistic and pessimistic scenarios? Your business plan must be specific and include the required activities and tasks necessary for you to be successful. You will need the product or service, the marketing plan, sales strategy, advertising and staffing requirements if any. You will essentially need all the planning

elements of a large company or organization but only on a smaller scale. Your business plan results must indicate adequate cash flows and earnings to sustain it as a viable business.

4. Do you have the needed capital to get started and sustain yourself for the projected needed timeframe? One of the major reasons small businesses fail is the lack of start-up capital due to underestimating what it will really take to get started. By the same token, having too much initial capital can be a problem as you might have a tendency to spend more than you should just because you have the capital available.

5. Have you made provisions for the possible benefits you might loose because of leaving your current employment? One of the fears or perceived risks sited was the concern about providing family benefits for things such as health care, life insurance and retirement plans adequate for long-term economic survival. This was sited as a major reason many did not follow their dream of business ownership. Traditionally, large companies have been able to negotiate favorable arrangements in this area.

6. Are you self motivated and committed to doing the very hard work required to run your own business? Anyone who believes that self-employment means more leisure time has not gotten the right message. When owning your own business, you will be required to hit the floor running each morning and will likely have very long days. The buck will always stop with you.

7. Do you welcome a major challenge? You will likely have multiple challenges to deal with no matter what type of business venture you are considering. Some days you will feel that everything that could go wrong has gone wrong.

8. Are you immune to low-level tasks? Whether you have employees or are going it alone, chances are you will be required to do some perceived low-level tasks. If you have a cleaning service, the day might come when you have to roll up your sleeves and clean. If you have prepared a strategic plan as part of your consulting practice, you might have to type the report or produce the power point presentation before presenting it to your client.

9. Do you have the support of family, friends, and the community? You will certainly need support from the people and organizations that are your support structure. Your family will be required to make sacrifices of your time and possibly financially due to cash flow requirements.

10. Do you possess the diversified skills required to run your own business? Large businesses have an organizational structure comprised of departments and/or work units. No matter what the size of your business or operation, you will be required to perform all business functions with the only difference being smaller numbers. You must have business plans, accounting, cost management, treasury, accounts payable, accounts receivable, tax strategy planning, and procurement. The depth and degree of knowledge and time associated with these activities will vary depending on your business type, size, and degree of complexity.

11. Can your business idea and the financial projections support your financial needs? If your initial evaluation does not indicate financial success, do not get discouraged. This just might mean that there is a need to modify your plans or strategies. Keep the plans realistic and achievable but identify changes in the tactics in order to deliver satisfactory financial results. Never result to forcing the financial numbers you desire because that would get you started down a path you should not travel.

If business ownership is your dream, follow that dream. Prepare yourself for the challenge and go for it. Often, the biggest risk in life is the risk not taken. Take failure out of your vocabulary and focus on the things needed to make you successful. I have witnessed many business plans in action, the successful ones had champions, and other supporters who believed the results could be accomplished. Remember that the keys to success in your new business endeavor will be people, business strategy, and the ability to execute.

Are You Getting What You Want From Your Career

Career strategies and plans can be beneficial as guidelines for aiding you in getting what you want from your career. In order to make those plans work, you must review and evaluate them with personal candor with the objective of making changes when needed. When thinking about where you are in your career, ask yourself the following questions and be prepared to change in order to get what you want.

1. Are you realizing what you have defined as success in your career?

2. Do you feel totally energized and ready to face the current and future challenges that will come from your career or profession?

3. Are you satisfied with the progress you have made in your business or organization? Do you see your progress continuing at satisfactory levels?
4. Do you enjoy being around the individuals you are required to interface with in your chosen profession?
5. Do you like and enjoy your physical location?
6. Do you have adequate time to spend with family and friends in order to achieve the needed balance in your life?
7. Are you continuing to learn and grow in your career or profession?
8. Is your compensation level adequate to satisfy your financial needs?
9. Are you satisfied with your potential in your profession and/or organization?
10. Do you like what you see in the mirror each morning when you think about how you have developed, committed to be your very best, and focused on achieving your goals and career aspirations?

Be totally true to yourself when evaluating and managing your career options. You must like the person you have become in order to have the satisfaction you need and deserve. If you do not like the course you are on, it is up to you to change and make the needed adjustments. In many instances, it will require some level of sacrifice, which means you have a defining moment and decisions to make if you are to improve your situation. You must keep your career moving forward by focusing on your goals, learning and contributing each day, gowning personally and professionally, adding value to your organization and making a difference. You cannot allow your career to reach a certain level and just stop growing. If it reaches a certain level and just stops, you will begin to decline. Things will change and your skills will become obsolete. Your career success will be driven by defining moments and decisions you will personally make. Make the right choices and you will have a satisfying career.

Phase IV: Personal Brand and Behavior

Chapter Fifteen:
Defining Who You Are

Keep away from people who try to belittle your ambitions. Small people always do that, but the really great make you feel that you, too, can become great.

Mark Twain

Your technical preparation, career selection process, on the job performance and personal career strategies all set the stage for the degree of success you will experience in your career. Your behavior will complete your package as a professional. Your objective should be to do the behavioral things that will separate you from the pack and make you special. People who exemplify outstanding behavior are the ones referred to as having it, has the look or acts and dresses the part. They light up the room and are a magnet to others in most any environment. You enjoy having a conversation with them and they can effectively communicate on a variety of subjects without dominating. Others like and enjoy being around them and see them as team players.

You must be in control of how you are defined in order to control how others will perceive you. You will be defined during your career by the choices you make and the things you do. Everyone you interface with will develop their opinions about you based on your appearance, your actions, and the things you do or fail to do. This will be the case for your customers, bankers, managers, employees, employers, peers, and associates of all types. There are no exceptions; everyone whom you will interface with will have an impression about you and your personal brand. These impressions will be either beneficial or detrimental to you for achieving your career and personal objectives.

When you have a positive brand, people will want to do business with you, they will want to be on your team or have you as a part of their team.

We have all grown up knowing how to recognize these people and how they are typically described. Positive brands are recognized by statements such as: he or she knows their stuff, they get things done, are dependable, delivers what is needed and more, does what they said they would do, goes beyond the call of duty and etc. Having positive traits and being able to do things, which others cannot accomplish, will be extremely valuable to you during your career. Develop this positive brand early in your career and it will deliver great rewards.

Avoid those negative brands such as being late for meetings, not delivering on assignments, inability to get along with others, not technically competent, not doing what you said you would, can not be counted on to support the team, does not take projects or assignments seriously and does not see his or her career as a priority. Those brands are negative and once you get them, it is often impossible to change those impressions. I have found that decision makers will typically avoid individuals who have negative brands. Hiring managers see these individuals as a chance not worth taking.

Most of us grew up with someone telling us to get your foot into the door of a desirable organization and you will be just fine. That is only partially true. That will get you a paycheck for some period but that might be all you have achieved. That is only the beginning of the journey toward getting the career you want and deserve. You must do those value added, exceptional things that make you special and define who you are as a person and professional. That will aid in separating you from the pack and assist you in having the brand you desire.

First impressions are powerful and do have an impact. They influence the professional perceptions you reflect and how you are defined. Respected studies indicate that judgments about people are made within the first four seconds of a new encounter. Lasting impressions are made in the first three to four minutes of initial contact. We spend the rest of the time we know the person, whether it is a day or a lifetime, reinforcing or changing those initial impressions. This does not mean those judgments are right or wrong, but does mean that they have been made and influenced how others will perceive you.

When you meet someone for the first time, over ninety percent of how you are judged is based on non-verbal data. Less than ten percent of that judgment is based on what you say. We have all heard or said things reflective of how these quick judgments are made. She or he spoke with confidence. He or she makes a good impression. I could see myself working with him/her. She or he would raise the quality of the department. I cannot put my finger on what it was but he or she was special. Those first impressions are made based on real data that you can control and manage. You should make every effort to manage the factors affecting your initial impressions.

Gloria Starr, a noted image consultant, says, "You do have a measure of control over how people react to you in those first few moments. Charming people look you directly in the eye in those first few crucial moments; alarming people avoid eye contact or look at you in a nervous way. Charming people smile when they first meet you; alarming people create distrust and anxiety with their serious and worried facial expressions. Charming people use open and receptive body language; alarming people set barriers with their body language and distrust sets in." When attempting to build instant rapport, you should use direct eye contact, smile, introduce yourself, shake hands, and ask open-ended questions to stimulate discussion. Your body language also impacts those impressions so you should use good posture, use open gestures, lean slightly forward toward the person, avoid crossing your arms or legs and use slow, fluid movements. These relatively simple actions can aid you immensely in establishing a good, positive first impression.

Once engaged, avoid those negative attributes that impact the impression others have of you such as being self-centered, closed minded, judgmental, using poor manners, poor conversational ability, negative life attitude, indecisive, whining and complaining and power games or manipulation. You do not want negative attributes to reinforce your brand. Think about the kind of people you enjoy being around and become that person. Do not allow those quick, subconscious judgments to destroy your chances for a successful career. Focus on those positive attributes that signal you really are approachable. Be warm and engaging. Send good body language and speak in a pleasant tone. Make your first impressions positive and doors to opportunity will open.

Defining moments happen all the time, many of which we never realize until much later or possibly never. They come in the form of chance meetings, the near misses, the chance introductions, and trouble or accident avoidance due to being five minutes early or late. We just do not know when they will occur which leaves the feeling of being unable to control or influence them. When thinking about this and reflecting on my parent tapes, I believe there are many things influencing our defining moments. The advice that we are given by our parents and others who care about us set the stage for the things we do without thinking about them. I can hear my mother saying many of the things we all need in order to prepare us for those instinctive reactions we make without even thinking about them. "Make sure you know who you are associating with, or you should stay out of that environment or pick your friends carefully." Looking back on those many conversations, they reveal clues to how our behavior is shaped. Those silent messages influence the chance meetings, the near misses and yes, the positive things that shape our lives and careers. We file our experiences and life messages for future use when we need the recall to influence our actions. Listen to your parent tapes, they will provide information and direction. They will influence your defining moments.

Chapter Sixteen:
Change Agent and Being the Standard

People are always blaming circumstances for what they are. I do not believe in circumstances. The people who get on in this world are the people who get up and look for the circumstances they want, and if they cannot find them, make them.

George Bernard Shaw

Individuals who are innovators and change agents improve their odds for career success when they create incremental value. This is true for entrepreneurs, employees, professionals of all types or any other form of career endeavor. These traits will be reflective off how you perform when striving to make processes, techniques, and/or services better. This is one of the many benefits of keeping your skills contemporary by learning continuously. Combine this with initiative and you are well on your way to success. Innovators will be valued in any organization or profession. All products and services have life cycles. Innovation is the only way to perpetually keep ahead of the competition and deliver productive solutions. Never let your products or services become commodities, that is the formula for becoming average. Keep your products and services fresh and you will be constantly in demand. I cannot think of any long-term organization, product, process, or profession that has not changed over time.

My experience with change during my business career has taught me important lessons. I have seen individuals and organizations resist change with all their resources. I have come to the realization that innovative, value added, market driven change cannot be stopped. It is like water flowing down a river; it can be diverted or slowed down but it cannot be permanently stopped. Market forces in our capitalistic system are efficient and will deliver those value added solutions, it is only a matter of time. That is why it is critical for those who desire to remain relevant and competitive in their career field must embrace change. Individuals who do this are constantly evolving and reinventing themselves by the things they do.

Resisting change is a learned behavior because most individuals have found and like their comfort zone. We seek and like what we feel is known and secure, our comfort zone. Change causes us to feel uneasy and we experience stress and tension. Change, if extreme enough, can affect our mental and physical health. That is why most of us take few chances and resist change if possible. This has been learned so well that it does not require thought; it is a natural response due to life long learning. That is why we seem to need a clear reason or a significant event in order for change to occur. There are theories that change only occurs when the pain of staying the same is greater than the pain of change. That might be true but it is not appropriate behavior. You cannot make progress if you are not willing to change.

We must all be prepared for and embrace change during our careers. The rate of change has been significant in the past and the rate of change is only going to increase in the future. Just think about the number of things that have changed over the past few years that affected how we live today. A few things that come to mind are cellular phones, ATM machines, personal computers, automobile navigation systems, DVD players and recorders, information available via the internet, electronic data transfer, electronic banking, on line investing and the list seems endless. The future rate of change will be even more dramatic than what has been experienced.

The very positive aspect of change is the elimination or a significant reduction in burnout in organizations because of doing and learning new things. Most situations involving change will generate more opportunities than they eliminate for those willing to accept the new challenges. Those who embrace the changes early are likely to be the beneficiary of those new opportunities. I am mindful of two major technology system conversions I was personally involved in and the opportunities there were for those who embraced the change early in the process. The two systems, which come to mind, are PeopleSoft's human resources and the SAP business management system. Trust me; there were numerous reasons why both of these new applications were going to happen. Several organizations reluctantly made the change and did so after openly resisting. My organization embraced the new systems from day one. We saw the benefits and wanted to be in the early wave of installations. The new systems had numerous benefits associated with productivity and the ability to generate real time data. We would be able to do and achieve things that previously had not been possible.

Numerous new career opportunities would be available for the people who acquired new skills derived from this state-of-the-art technology.

A number of individuals involved in the early conversions were candidates for positions that were now available in other areas of the business and industry. This technology was new and the system conversions were just beginning. New positions were created for trainers, system administrators, user experts, control facilitators, data maintenance specialist, quality assurance management, and programmers. It also created positions for process experts in recognition that you should not put new technology over old processes. I am sure you agree that many new opportunities are being created for those who embraced the new systems. Learn to dance with change by embracing new and innovative ways to perform your functions. Take advantage of change and use it to your strategic advantage during your career; you will be pleased with the results.

One of the best and most effective ways of promoting your personal brand is by becoming the standard by which others are measured. Those are the people identified as being best in class. They are the individuals peers go to informally when they need direction and advice. These individuals are looked at as second in command in the organization. Achieving this level of peer respect is certainly self-assuring regarding your abilities. I know I was and feel that you will as well when embraced in this way. It says that you are special and that is what you want during your career.

When you set the standard or better still, raise the bar, you do not accept your job or current position for what it has been in the past. You strive to make it better and more valuable to the organization or your business enterprise. You bring new and improved ideas or approaches to the organization. That is the only way organizations continuously improve which is essential in any competitive environment. You do this by taking calculated risks and not being afraid to try new ideas and approaches. This keeps organizations ahead of the competition; it is essential for success. Individuals who facilitate this are needed and valued.

When you are valued, you will be respected and compensated for what you do and contribute. When you accomplish something special, it is your responsibility to make sure your value is recognized. Do not keep what you have done a secret. You do this by making sure your brand is adequately promoted. Use your written communication skills to write good reports about your work and its results. Use your presentation skills to convey your messages about what you have done. Work to be published in internal bulletins and external trade association's publications or magazines. This will promote your brand while being an asset to your networking activities. It will also be a lot of fun and a good diversion from your normal duties and responsibilities. You never know when you will make a positive impression on someone important to your future success. Never leave the promotion of your personal brand to others; it just might not happen the way you would like. Take personal charge of this important responsibility and make sure it happens.

Chapter Seventeen:
Ethics–Putting it All Together

Each time you are honest and conduct yourself with honesty, a success force will drive you toward greater success. Each time you lie, even with a little white lie, there are strong forces pushing you toward failure.

Joseph Sugarman

When I was very young, my father taught me that you should always tell the truth. He reasoned that if you tell one lie, you would likely have to tell another and another after that to the point that you no longer can relate and identify with the truth. You would eventually forget something you had said and all the untruths would be exposed. He reasoned that you would no longer be able to distinguish the difference between fiction and the truth. That is a lesson I learned early in life which carried over into my business career. It was the foundation of my operating with the highest degree of honesty and integrity and for that, I am eternally grateful. I never saw value or benefit from doing things that were not ethically sound. I hope that you have or will develop the quality of virtue; it will serve you well in any profession.

Think of this relative to the business scandals involving Enron, Arthur Andersen, Tyco, World Com, and others. I have heard comments such as, I hope this situation has not started us down a slippery slope, or when you are in a hole, the first thing you must do is stop digging. Those comments are essentially equivalent to the advice my dad gave me years ago. That is why I feel so good that I developed the belief that the truth is the only appropriate position. My guidance is that you adopt the philosophy and practice of being truthful in all your personal and professional dealings. Never compromise on this principle and you will avoid a number of potential problems and embracing situations. If the issues are significant enough, they could lead to potential criminal actions, as has been the case for many of the recent corporate scandals. You do not want to find yourself in that unfortunate situation.

Most organizations will have policies and procedures that reflect operating with a responsible code of ethics. However, as a professional, you should not have to depend on those policies and procedures to provide you direction. You must do the right thing reflective of your personal integrity; do not rely on it being legislated. If you are requested to do something by an individual in authority that is clearly illegal, dishonest and in violation of ethical principles, you are faced with a defining moment. Moments like these define who you are as a professional. Make the decision that you know is the right one and never compromise your integrity.

Many of the scandals in business, industry, and government are often believed to be the fault of poor leadership. They are often thought of as having a chain of command that just was not effective. That is certainly partially true but there is another point of view. Another way of looking at these failings is a lack of individual responsibility. Individuals have to shoulder responsibility and be accountable for their actions. Professionals step up and take responsibility for the things they do or fail to do. They have been trained and certainly know the difference between right and wrong. Individuals must learn to lead themselves; that is one of the foundations of self-directed work teams. It recognizes the need for and importance of individual accountability and its place in high performing organizations. This requires that individuals do what is appropriate and be willing to take responsibility for their actions.

This also recognizes the importance of having individuals in organizations that have the courage to speak up when problems occur. Audits help with the control process but they should not be depended on to enforce honesty. They do not stop inappropriate things from happening because they occur after the fact. They identify what has already occurred, when the auditors get lucky. High performing organizations prevent damaging actions from occurring. Those organizations have an effective culture and people with the courage to do the right thing. They do not need supervision in order to know what is right versus wrong. These people will put their character above personal short-term gain whenever there is a choice. This is one of the traits you must have to be viewed as an outstanding performer. One compromise in the area of ethics can destroy a thriving career. It does not matter how much good you have done in the past or what your potential is for the future. Virtue is a trait you must have as a professional.

Defining who you are and managing your personal brand requires sustained and specific actions on your part just as it does for any product or service. You want to be the person that is respected for your abilities and positive qualities. I hope you recognize the importance of a positive brand and the career benefits that will result. Your brand is important and it is up to you to manage it for maximum benefit. Use the following six action items to increase your personal brand acceptance.

1. **Know thy self:** Know your strengths, unique professional qualities, special skills and the things that make you special. Be able to express how your skills will be an asset to any organization. Raise the bar by doing things others cannot or will not do.

2. **Know what you want**: Know the things you are motivated to do and your passion. This will create the enthusiasm needed to sustain you throughout your career. Identify the goals you plan to achieve over the next five to ten years and beyond. Dream big and believe you are worthy.

3. **Be committed:** Knowing what you want without being committed will get you nothing. Focus on the things you want to achieve and stay the course by being totally committed to goal accomplishment.

4. **Deliver results**: Focus on and deliver value added results for your organization. Be dependable and the person the organization can depend on to get things done.

5. **Be there**: You must be visible in order to support and defend your brand. You cannot do that by being out of touch and absent from the visible platforms. Attend the meetings, social events, seminars, and external functions that will give you the needed exposure to those with influence. Those are the stages, which will launch your career in the direction you desire. Show up and actively participate; just being there is not enough.

6. **Do not disappoint:** Under promise and over deliver or at a minimum; never disappoint. Leaders like and appreciate positive surprises and can not accept negative surprises. Communicate and do all within your power to deliver on your commitments.

Build your positive brand and enjoy the many benefits that will be afforded you. Do those things that will clearly separate you from the pack. Positive branding is an asset in all professions. To put this into perspective, think about some of the public figures you know something about and identify those with positive brands and those with negative brands. After doing this, develop your personal opinion of how you feel each is valued and respected in their organizations or by the public. My guess is that you would rather be associated with those who you feel have positive brands.

Chapter Eighteen:
Professional Etiquette and Behavior

You make yourself and others suffer just as much when you take offense as when you give offense.

Ken Keyes, Jr.

Your technical skills and abilities might get you hired but without practicing good etiquette, your promotional potential will be limited. You must reflect the appropriate image in order to be favorably accepted by those you interface with in your profession. I say they might get you hired because I have seen candidates rejected at various stages of the selection process due to poor etiquette. I am sure many of these candidates never knew the real reason why they had been rejected. You can bet the individuals participating in the interview data integration sessions knew and shared the real reasons for the rejections. That is unfortunate because when you do not know the things that are holding you back; you cannot address them and move forward. I firmly believe most people will do better when they know better and that is certainly true about etiquette.

Etiquette is the code of unwritten expectations that govern social behavior. It usually reflects a theory of conduct that society or traditions have invested heavily in over time. Etiquette fundamentally concerns the ways in which people interact with each other and show their respect for other people by conforming to the norms of society. Violations of etiquette, if severe, can cause hurt feelings, misunderstandings, or real grief and pain. It would reasonably be correct to view etiquette as the politically correct actions required to avoid major conflict in polite society.

Etiquette is not something we are born with; it must be learned and practiced until it becomes your natural behavior. If you have any concern at all regarding your level of etiquette understanding, do yourself possibly the best favor of your life by getting the needed training. Poor etiquette can destroy the careers of otherwise very talented people with many never knowing what the specific problems are that are holding them back. One of the reasons for this is the difficulty most individuals have with discussions on this subject with friends, relatives, employees, peers and other associates. No one likes or find it easy to deliver this type message so the problems my never be addressed. Outstanding technical people frequently are passed over for promotions without being told the real reason they were not chosen for available positions. Some are given a fabricated reason just to end the discussion.

True friends and good managers need to be honest with those they care about when they feel personal etiquette is an issue. Managers or leaders should do it for the person as well as their organization. People are what the internal and external world sees and you should project the best possible image at all times. Friends should communicate etiquette issues because of your caring relationship and concern that the individual is not becoming the best they can be. Anyone delivering this type message should do so with kindness, dignity, and respect. No one appreciates being unnecessarily put down so be sensitive if you feel there is a need to express feelings about etiquette issues. You do this by not only what you say, but also how and where it is said, the tone and the preparation before the message is conveyed. It would be nice to have a mutual agreement with two or more individuals with open permission to provide constructive feedback and comments in areas of improvement. I would suggest praising as a part of the process because no one can handle constant criticism. If you always deliver criticism, others will soon avoid or regret seeing you. Have balance in your comments by mixing them with some positives.

My intent was to raise your awareness about the importance of etiquette in career success, and I hope that has been accomplished. Since this is an extremely important and broad area, I would suggest you invest in at least one good book on etiquette for your personal library. The areas covered will be dressing appropriately, personal and professional conduct, proper manners, greetings, sending and responding to invitations, expressing appreciation, table manners, and a host of other traditional as well as contemporary topics on behavior. There will also be information regarding etiquette in the information age as we do more things electronically and via multi media processes. The book I personally like is *"New Manners for New Times"* by Letitia Baldrige. You will be able to use it as a quick reference when you need assurance, have a question, or any doubt regarding etiquette or appropriate behavior in personal or business situations.

You can also find a wealth of information on the subject of etiquette on the internet. The traditional things do not change but new items are added as our operating environments change and evolve. The new global impact of etiquette is evolving all the time and this requires a completely different level of sensitivity. A couple of web sites I would recommend for information and possible training in this area are www.GloriaStarr.com or www.executiveplanet.com . Practicing good etiquette skills will certainly enhance your personal brand and ultimately your career. Good etiquette is needed at all professional levels, and it gets increasingly critical the higher you rise in your chosen profession. The earlier it is practiced, the better, as you cannot afford to wait for executive training. You will need good etiquette to have hopes of getting to that level. Get training in this critical area that traditionally does not receive the level of attention and focus it deserves, if there is a need.

Time Management

Good time management skills are essential in any career or profession. It will influence how effective and efficient you will be in performing your functions. There are very few careers where individuals do not have choices regarding the things they will do each day. Good time management is a combination of common sense, techniques, and experience over time to develop these skills. Most people feel that they have more to do than time available. When this happens, frustration, guilt and stress can be the outcome. Time management skills will not eliminate the pressures and conflicts that arise in the work environment but it should make the workday more satisfying and pleasant. Consider the following to aid you in evaluating how proficient you are in managing your time:

- ✓ Are you handling the things you really do not like early in the day to avoid procrastination and them staying in the back of your mind?
- ✓ Have you prioritized your time to address the high value items?
- ✓ Have you identified the things that are preventing you from being productive?
- ✓ Do you start each day with a clear vision of what you want to achieve?
- ✓ Do you have the feeling of being organized and in control of your work?

Following are the things you should consider to improve in the area of time management:

- ✓ Have clear and defined objectives for your responsibilities.
- ✓ Plan your time based on the things you need to do and do everything possible to eliminate interruptions.

✓ Have a calendar and action list that is current.
✓ Get organized and have your work area working with and not against you.
✓ Watch out for those time wasters and avoid them.
✓ Communicate effectively with those you must work with.
✓ Learn to say no to requests that do not move you toward goal attainment.

Time management skills are essential for those desiring to perform at high levels in any career or profession. This skill will result in you achieving more than others who are less organized and not able to manage their time effectively. The earlier you develop these skills in your career, the better. Let them become your natural way of operating. My experience tells me that being on time for meetings and appointments is critical for those desiring to send a very positive signal about who you are as a person and professional. Develop the habit of planning to be early as your insurance policy for never being late for an appointment. Once you establish this trait as a priority, it will be with you for the remainder of your career and life. If you do not develop this habit, you will at some point in your career, experience an embarrassing moment that will not be pleasant. Good time management is one of the most positive traits you can have as a professional.

Conduct at Social Events

Your conduct at a social event or holiday party can destroy an outstanding career that is moving forward. What you say and do at these events can leave a lasting impression. It only takes seconds for those impressions to be made, make them positive. In thinking about this, I instantly recall an incident at an event when an outstanding information technology professional decided he would drink flaming ouzo. He proceeded to light the drink and accidentally set his mustache on fire. For the next year or so, that was his defining moment. He was no longer known as an outstanding information technology professional. He was now branded as the person who set his mustache on fire. This occurred over 20 years ago and I can see the event like it was yesterday. That is how lasting the action was for me and I am sure it was the same for others who witnessed the act. Think about this and the likely significant change in your career potential before you decide to put that lampshade on your head or dance on the piano at the next office social function. You do not want some inappropriate behavior to become your defining moment.

I suggest you seriously consider your behavior before attending social events or parties. Social situations can be valuable and enhancing to your career when used appropriately. In order to capitalize on the benefits, you must avoid embarrassing actions such as rude jokes, drunken behavior, or leering at a co-workers spouse. Save yourself some career pain after those parties by doing the following:

1. If you drink alcohol, set a limit and stick to it.
2. Wear appropriate clothes.
3. Keep your hands to yourself.
4. Stay away from telling jokes.
5. Use good etiquette at all times.
6. Know when it is time to leave the party. The longer you stay, the greater the chance you will say or do something that is inappropriate.

Never, use a social setting to either give or receive feedback on performance. This is also not your chance to set the record straight with your boss or a co-worker. That is not the appropriate setting and you have increased your odds of saying something you might later regret. Consider using a partner system as a safeguard for your conduct at social functions, you both might benefit from the arrangement. If you are getting a little loud or beginning to act inappropriately, your partner can call it to your attention and possibly suggest that it is time to leave. You can do the same for your partner, which creates a win/win situation. The following are what I call career-limiting mistakes I feel you should avoid at social events:

1. **Position does not have privilege:** Always treat your subordinates, peers, and superiors with dignity and respect. Your manager or supervisor should not ask you and you should not ask a subordinate to perform tasks such as getting drinks or food, retrieve coats or giving up their seats.
2. **Never criticize your spouse or significant other**: Show respect for the person you have chosen to accompany you to the affair. Do not use this as your opportunity to talk about all of the frugal things the finance person does such as using coupons, buying from bargain stores, or using generic brands.
3. **Gossip:** All things and all people fit in this off limit area. The world is very small and you should not take a chance of potentially offending someone.

4. **Do not complain:** Never complain about the food, venue, or other guests. You are special; you have been chosen as a guest. Show appreciation and respect.

5. **Manage conversations:** Do not wear your religious and political views on your shoulder. We are living in diverse times and there are different opinions on both religion and politics. Social events are not the forum for getting resolution on either of these topics. Your chances of offending are much greater than consensus or resolution.

6. **Be considerate:** Leave the kids at home. If you do not, you will be one of the event conversation pieces but you will not like the things being said. No one will sympathize with your baby sitters movie commitment, cold, or football game. Find an alternative other than bringing kids to an adult event.

Make social events memorable but do not feel like you need to be remembered by doing something that is out of bounds. You do not need those negative labels when it is time for the next promotion or major project opportunity. Once you demonstrate negative behavior, the only question is when the behavior will be repeated. It is okay to be the life of the party but make that lasting memory positive by all that you say and do. Remember that those defining moments can happen anytime and many only take a few seconds to become lasting impressions.

Expressing Appreciation

One of the clear messages I received while doing my research for this book was that people want to feel appreciated. They like recognition for the things they do that are special or above normal expectations. This was true for all levels, career types, and professions. People feel good about positive reinforcements and like the satisfaction of having someone validate them as a professional. We enjoy the feeling of success and the recognition we get from others no matter how short and sweet the message. The impact of those messages last for a very long time.

I will never forget the first recognition letter I received for a significant promotion and that was over 30 years ago. I had been promoted to the Finance Manager position of a manufacturing facility for a fortune 500 company. I had become the youngest department manager in that facility and possibly the entire company. It required a move to a new location and I would have people to manage for the fist time in my professional career. Naturally, there was a certain amount of anxiety even though I felt prepared. When I opened my first letter of congratulations, I could feel the confidence build. It seemed that having someone else express confidence and best wishes was refreshing and validated my personal confidence. After reading that letter, I began to feel like everything would be just fine.

I kept that letter for years and never forgot the individual who thought enough to send it. The kind words left a lasting impression. I witnessed how it made me feel and it increased my level of sensitivity we all should have to others. People do remember and appreciate the acts of kindness expressed by others. They can also benefit you personally in your career, as I am sure I was a little more sensitive to Ron when he called after my next promotion. He was a plant manager at a facility for which I had functional finance responsibility. He likely got the benefit of some favorable decisions whenever I had to make decisions about his facilities and organization.

When you feel the need to express your pleasure to someone for an accomplishment, do it with a special touch. Do not just send an electronic message as you would for any routine correspondence. Make it special by sending a hand written note, addressed by you personally and with a postage stamp and not a postage meter. You want some things to be special so treat them as such. Just think about how you would personally feel when receiving this type communication. It obviously means someone cares enough to use their personal time communicating. It will be received positively and will certainly be appreciated and remembered.

Your behavior will be the actions that put the closure on your performance as a professional. Your behavior completes your package and puts you on the road to success. Look at your behavior as your career finishing school. Use these skills effectively and they will be a major strategic advantage that will make you special. These are skills that you will find useful in both your personal and professional life.

Career Assessments

Success on any major scale requires you to accept responsibility...in the final analysis, the one quality that all successful people have...is the ability to take on responsibility.

Michael Korda

Given that my primary motivation for writing this book was to give individuals improved skills for managing their careers, I felt compelled to utilize my survey to receive input from over 50 individuals who had years of relatively successful career experience. I wanted to know what lessons they had learned from their career experiences. Some had their share of issues to deal with but that is reality. I feel you will gain from hearing what they had to say and that their comments will aid you in your career choices. They were generally content with the level of success they had achieved to this point but realized they had gained wisdom and was willing to share what they had learned. Even the respondent, who felt very content with and would not give up the career and life he had experienced, felt that if he could have another, he would do things differently. He would pursue a career that would have a broader impact on society, possibly in the medical research area. Therefore, even the content individuals have things to offer as guidance. That thought was consistent with the giving nature of these individuals. Most were driven by what they were motivated to do and not by money and other financial rewards.

Another revelation from the responses was that some might interpret this as meaning correcting things that might have been wrong. For example, consider decisiveness. Is too much or to little right or wrong? Leadership; should you always lead or are there times when it is appropriate and more effective to follow? I think the lesson I learned from this input was that it is important to consider how you act and behave in different situations to see if it is effective or ineffective as opposed to how you might naturally react.

Dr. Robert Houston put this question in perspective by saying, "Living life over again, I would be more aware that luck plays more of a role than we would all like to believe. However, do not live your life as if luck plays a big role. Do not take counsel from those who seem very lucky; who dream walk through life with no ill effects who say relax, life will take care of itself nor from those who seem to always be unlucky who say whatever can go bad, goes bad. You must do the things in life that will improve your odds of being the success you desire."

The entrepreneurial spirit was very high from the respondents. Several owned businesses or were considering leaving the corporate world to start a business. Some of the business ventures had been successful and some had failed. Each of the business owners who had failed by the common definition really had not. Each of them had learned significantly from their experiences. Some had started another business in the same or a different field with varying degrees of success. If you have no failures, you probably are not doing very much or doing things that are not very challenging. Failure, to some degree, is all a part of being successful.

It is critical that we gain from the experiences of others when trying to improve, and career management is no exception. There were a number of consistent messages in response to my survey when I asked the respondents to complete the statement: "If I could live my life over, as it relates to my career, I would…," The summary responses I received follow:

✓ Gotten broader overall experience
✓ Been less egocentric and aggressive
✓ Gotten an advanced degree earlier
✓ Followed entrepreneurial dreams earlier
✓ Developed stronger skills
✓ Adjusted behavior to fit specific situations
✓ Made more career changes
✓ Been more focused
✓ Been less stubborn and opinionated
✓ Taken more risks
✓ Been more balanced between work and life
✓ Would not have taken all career situations personally
✓ Been more flexible and liberally educated as the future is too unknown
✓ Been more candid with employees and listened to everyone

In reality, none of us will live life over. We are all a product of our many experiences and the things we learn from others. I hope that this input from seasoned professionals will aid you with the many choices you will make during your career. While your career will be different from any combination of those surveyed, there were a number of comments that should provide insight and value. It is up to each of us to learn from others and avoid following paths that do not deliver the satisfying results we desire.

Strategic Career Messages to Live By

I've missed more than 9000 shots in my career. I've lost almost 300 games. 26 times, I've been trusted to take the game winning shot and missed. I've failed over and over and over again in my life. And that is why I succeed.

Michael Jordan

It is my hope that this book will leave the readers with ideas, concepts, and specific actionable items that will deliver more successful and rewarding careers. I have researched and given personal thought to the key factors that affect the success and failures during careers. Solutions for many of these are embellished in the various sections of this book. In addition to that, I felt it would be beneficial to summarize many of these items as a potential quick reference to stimulate action for goal accomplishment. I hope you will find the summary, which follows, helpful as you focus on achieving your career objectives or for helping others whom you have responsibility for providing guidance and counsel.

1. Find a mentor, hopefully one inside your current organization and one outside that organization. Being mentored by the right person is an important and vital element for success. The mentor guides his or her protégé in developing skills, methods and work habits, which the mentor developed over his or her entire career. The mentor becomes, in effect, the portal to the business experts and resources the protégé will need for professional growth and development.

2. Plan to arrive early for business meetings and functions. If the function begins at 8:00 AM, arrive at 7:45 AM at the latest. You will have time to relax and relieve anxiety, network, read the pulse of other attendees, identify supporters or adversaries, collect your thoughts and fine tune any last minute adjustments you need to make before the meeting begins. Moreover, you certainly do not

want to establish the negative brand of being late for meetings. Make the attention you get positive and never negative.

3. If you have not already done so, develop the habit of getting adequate sleep and start your day early. You will feel refreshed and ready for your activities of the day. Arrive early at your work location and you will accomplish more before others arrive and the distractions begin to occur. Additionally, you are sending a message that your career is important to you and your life's work is a priority.

4. Know thyself! Get to know who you are by conducting a thorough, honest appraisal of your strengths and your weaknesses. Begin using your strengths for all possible advantage while concurrently working on your weaknesses as best you can. Be mindful that circumstances can sometimes change the perception of strengths and perceived weaknesses. Know the difference between things that are legitimate performance concerns versus personality differences or perceptions.

5. Plan for your annual performance evaluation all year long. Keep accurate records of your accomplishments and their impact on the organization. Make sure you use this opportunity to set the stage for the future by discussing your career aspirations. Give this process the attention it needs; it is much too important to be rushed or done without adequate preparation.

6. You can be sure that change will be a constant during your career. You will not be able to stop it and there are penalties for attempting to avoid or slow it down. Diversify your experiences and knowledge while embracing change. Every time one door closes, another will open for those who are prepared and have the right experiences and transferable skills.

7. When you make yourself needed, people will value you. When you are valued, you will be compensated for what you deliver. Constantly strive to increase your personal value by doing things others cannot or will not do. You will get more personal satisfaction while increasing your earning potential.

8. Always operate with the highest degree of honesty and integrity. This trait is non-negotiable. Violating this rule just once can destroy an outstanding career immediately. It does not matter how much good you have done in the past or how much you might be able to do in the future; it is over.

9. Train yourself to remain calm in seemingly difficult situations. You increase your odds of doing or saying something, you might

later regret if you get emotional. Keep all things in perspective and realize that there will always be another day. All things will pass.

10. If you must disagree with someone, learn to do so without being disagreeable. Most situations you will encounter during your career do not rise to the level of significance to justify destroying a personal or professional relationship.

11. Put effort into managing and promoting your personal brand. Never leave that responsibility to others; no one will ever have the same level of interest in your success.

12. Always be responsive in your personal and professional relationships. You have a chance to send a message each time you interact with others, send positive messages.

13. Create a personal mission statement. Review it frequently and keep it visible. Manage and follow-up on your career plan on a quarterly and/or annual basis to make sure you are on track to accomplish your career goals.

14. Have written goals that reflect the things you need to accomplish. You will need these no matter whether you are self-employed, an employee, or a contractor. Have a detailed daily action plan, which supports your goals in order to facilitate goal accomplishment.

15. We all have activities in our profession that we dislike and often avoid. Handle those things early in the day and move on to the things you have passion for and find rewarding.

16. If you need additional training in order to achieve your goals, get the training you need. Good performance is the result of continuous learning and development.

17. Keep your professional skills contemporary and your resume fresh. You never know when you will need to make a change so be prepared. Manage your career with the same discipline you would a business; it is essentially the same.

18. Have adequate balance in your life. That is required to support your needs and we all need ways of recharging and energizing ourselves.

19. Develop good health maintenance habits and make them a part of your normal routine. Without good health, your career achievements mean nothing.

20. Show that you are approachable by your body language. Others will get to know you while you expand your list of contacts. You never know when a chance encounter will lead to a great idea, valuable contact, or networking opportunity.

21. Do not depend on luck alone to achieve your career goals. Work on the factors that facilitate your luck; knowledge, skills, preparation, and contacts.

22. Relax and enjoy life. When you are rushed and stressed out, you are blind to opportunities and good fortune.

23. Read about and experience things you currently know nothing or little about. You just might discover something new and exciting. This is also a wonderful way to enhance your ability to have stimulating conversations during business, professional and social events.

24. Dream big! Expect good fortune, expect to achieve desired results and be sensitive to the psychology of performance. If you do not believe you can, you want. Nothing has ever been achieved when it was not believed possible.

25. Success in your career will be impacted by the things you do or fail to do. Learn to show up, be active, and contribute value.

26. Act and be positive in all that you do during your career. Negative attitudes can and will destroy an organization. It will eventually destroy you as well no matter whether you are a business owner, independent contractor or working for an organization as an employee. You always have choices so choose to be positive and never play that self-destructive *"isn't it awful"* game.

27. Learn to say and send those notes that say the simple words, *"thank you."* Do it sincerely when appreciation is deserved. You will feel good personally and those being recognized will be thrilled with this positive reinforcement.

28. When you achieve a leadership position, learn to delegate, but never ask more of your subordinates than you are personally willing to give. Respect must be earned and can never be demanded. Others will hear what you say but they will always watch your footprints to see what you do.

29. We will all have bumps in the road during our career. Do not let them be your defining moment, leave that to how you respond. Be mindful that all things will pass.

30. Be aware that during your career, "stuff will happen." There will be some people who will like or dislike you for no apparent reason. There is the potential for bad breaks to happen that have nothing to do with you personally or things that you can reasonably control. Manage your defining moments as best you can.

31. Travel, the world is getting smaller everyday and we all need to be exposed to and sensitive to other cultures and ways of thinking.

32. Choose carefully the people you allow to have a front row seat in your life, they will affect how you are defined as well as many of the choices you make.

33. You cannot be what you do not know. When you need training of any type in order to improve, get it.

34. Learn to take calculated risks; you might have the opportunity to get what you want out of life. Focus on the positives associated with risk and not the negatives that prevent us from taking action.

35. You need to know who you are and what you want. Define yourself and learn the things important for your personal success. Understand your options and be prepared to support the choices you make with passion.

36. Never depend on others to lead and guide your actions. Be professional and learn to lead yourself. That is the only way you will be able to control your destiny.

37. The higher you rise in an organization, the more you will be exposed to and required to handle sensitive, confidential information. Show that you can do so early in your career and never participate in the rumor mill. This will improve your odds of becoming a serious candidate for leadership positions.

38. Learn and practice good etiquette. Your technical skills and abilities might get you hired but without practicing good etiquette, your promotional potential will be limited. Practice polite conduct in all that you do.

39. Learn and practice humility no matter what level of success you achieve in life. Continue to treat all those you encounter with dignity and respect. Never forget that people and your relationships got you to where you are and they can bring you down.

40. We will all experience difficult times during our career; times when you feel others have done you wrong or have not treated you fairly. Those situations will be bumps in the road to success but never forget the lessons learned. They will make you stronger and more prepared for future career challenges.

41. Finally, follow your true dreams, do what you are passionate about, take calculated risks, discover, innovate, have fun, and enjoy the journey! Remember that 30 years from now; you will regret more the things you did not do during your career than the things you did. *"May the wind be always at your back."*

Conclusion:
Career Strategy Open Letter

Success can make you go one of two ways. It can make you a prima donna—or it can smooth the edges, take away the insecurities, and let the nice things come out.

Barbara Walters

You can have the career you want and deserve by implementing the strategies that have been identified. Your career will be impacted by the choices you make and your actions. Your choices will begin with the decision regarding the career opportunity you pursue. Begin this process by assessing what you are motivated to do and your passion. Do not leave this important decision to chance; put the required thought, research, and evaluation into the process to become comfortable with your decision. By choosing to do what you are motivated to do, you will increase your odds of selecting a career that will be personally satisfying and professionally rewarding.

Your next important decision will be deciding the structure, format, or type organization you chose as your affiliation. This could be in the form of business ownership for those who have the entrepreneurial spirit, an employee, independent contractor, consultant etc. You will need to research each area and decide what fits best with your personal style and abilities. If your plans are to join and affiliate with an organization, you will need a good understanding about that organization, its vision, mission, culture, businesses practices, processes and products or services. They must be compatible with your personal beliefs and convictions.

If you plan to work in a corporate environment, make sure you have a good understanding of its leadership and operating philosophies. Leadership does matter, it is essential to an organization's success. Leadership establishes the organization's culture and everything that flows from that culture. It creates the organization's vision, mission, and strategies and develops and/

or approves all operating plans and tactics. That is essentially all that the organization will or fails to do so never underestimate the importance that leadership will have on any organization. You must be comfortable with the organization's leadership and their abilities in order to have a successful and rewarding career.

While compensation is not everything, you should be comfortable with your rate of compensation. Do your research and know the value of what you bring to the organization. Conduct a detailed compensation comparison that is inclusive of all elements when evaluating multiple offers. Be sensitive to the non-cash compensation when determining total rewards. Those items can be significant and very costly if you are required to supply them as an individual or private business owner.

After making your required choices for your career type, performing must be your focus. Begin immediately to set the tone for who you are as a professional and never stop getting better. This will require that you are initially prepared and that you keep your skills contemporary by continuously learning. You will not be able to relax and believe that you have learned all you need to know during your career as things will change. New and developing skills will be a constant for your entire career. You must set goals and performance standards that will be monitored and measured to determine the progress you are making toward goal accomplishment. You must perform and deliver value no matter what profession you choose. It does not matter if you are a business owner or an employee; it is still value that will drive your level of success. Be dependable and deliver timely and high quality results.

Individuals who are innovative, decisive, resilient, trustworthy, team players, technically competent and self-motivated are in demand in all professions. These people get things done and add value to their organization or profession. They are in demand and will have rewarding careers. If you demonstrate some combination of these traits, you are well on your way to success. Learn to do these things, make them a natural part of your personal brand. Do what you say you will and never disappoint. If you must surprise, make it a pleasant surprise by delivering more than what was expected.

Make sure you know specifically how and by whom you will be evaluated. Know the written and unwritten rules about the performance evaluation process. If improvement areas are ever identified, address them immediately and do not let the situation get any worse. If you need additional training in order to improve, get that training immediately. You will be preparing yourself to function better in your current capacity while preparing for the future. Monitor your performance all year long in order to insure there are no surprises during the formal review session. Work to achieve a relationship with the individual you report to that facilitates continuous communication regarding performance and other topics of strategic importance.

Understand the logical career path for your chosen profession. Set your expectations high and never let anyone kill or distract you from your goals. Be prepared to take calculated risks and look at the positive side of risk in order to get what you want. Diversify your skills and be prepared for change. Be receptive to new opportunities and you never know when they will surface. You should stay open to non-traditional professions and positions during your career; they might offer some interesting and rewarding opportunities.

Mentoring is an important part of the career development process that you should consider. It can be your portal to success as it provides access to a wealth of experience that you will find of value. It will require active participation on the part of the mentor and the protégé in order to be effective. You should also actively network as it provides connections to opportunities, often before generally known. Managing your relationships will aid you in being connected to the right people and processes.

Be sensitive to the fact that everyone's time will come to make a change in what you have been doing. It could be by choice or for reasons of which you might not have a personal choice. In any case, be prepared to do what you must do to keep moving forward in your career. Learn to dance with change and embrace the many positive benefits of changing and doing something new and possibly much different. Anyway, it just makes since to test the market from time to time; you might find an attractive and exciting opportunity. Keep your resume fresh and up-to-date with your latest professional accomplishments and educational achievements.

If you encounter bumps in the road during your career, do not let them be your defining moment. How you react to the situation is what will make the difference. If you encounter a difficult manager or leader of any type, develop a strategy for dealing with the individual in the most effective way possible. You will certainly learn from the situation and become stronger as a result. Remember that all things will pass no matter how difficult they might seem.

Never let anyone define who you are, be defined by your values and actions. Make a good first impression and build on that impression during your entire career. Being defined as someone who delivers results by being technically competent, treating others with dignity and respect, has honesty and integrity and the courage to do the right thing are some of the most important traits.

Your behavior will be a major factor in how your career develops. Learn to be on time and manage your time for maximum productivity and efficiency. Be on your best professional behavior at all times, as you never know when a chance meeting or encounter might lead to an outstanding career opportunity. Dress the part and always practice good business and professional etiquette.

Have balance in your life, as work is not everything. You need to identify and allow time for those things that sustain you in order to be fulfilled and complete. Staying constantly at work will drain you and prevent you from being productive. Take the time you need in order to recharge your batteries. Career success with nothing else will not be very satisfying.

Stay true to your formula for success and do not get distracted. You must consistently do the things necessary in order to be successful; there are no short cuts. That is the way you will control your destiny. Be mindful that you can gain wisdom from others by watching what they do. History is a good predictor of the future so look at what successful individuals have done in order to improve your odds of success. I considered the traits possessed by a number of business, professional, government, academic, athletic, and entertainment professionals and many of them had a high percentage of the common traits. I encourage you to make your own list and see if you concur with my conclusions. The traits of the high performers I identify follow:

- ✓ They were all motivated to do what they did and had passion.
- ✓ They were all well prepared for their chosen field.
- ✓ They had tremendous focus and were not easily distracted.
- ✓ They openly embraced change.
- ✓ They learned continuously, worked hard, and always tried to get better.
- ✓ They had a positive, can do attitude.
- ✓ They showed tremendous patience.
- ✓ They were philanthropic and gave back in many ways.

You significantly improve your odds of success by doing the things that successful people do. Decide to commit yourself to doing the things that work in order to get what you want from your career. Believe that you are worthy of great things and never let anyone kill your dreams. The very best to you in your career endeavors.

Sincerely,

Robert

About the Author

Robert Donald was educated at North Carolina Agricultural and Technical State University. He has had post-graduate studies in business management, strategic business planning, total quality management, six sigma, strategic competitive advantage and numerous business, finance and technology related areas. He has had a successful 33 year career in business affiliations with fortune 500 companies. His corporate experience began as a financial analyst and he has held executive level positions in finance, marketing, business planning, manufacturing, auditing, and compensation and benefits. He has been an active participant in numerous industry and professional trade associations. After a successful corporate career, he became a successful entrepreneur with a business focus on strategic business planning and financial coaching. He is a frequent presenter to gatherings of professionals on the topic of career management and takes pleasure in one-on-one counseling with individuals desiring to improve their career situation. He lives in New Albany, Ohio.

Printed in the United States
104969LV00003B/234/A

9 781425 909604